# PENSION FUNDS
## A COMMONSENSE GUIDE
## TO A COMMON GOAL

# PENSION FUNDS
## A COMMONSENSE GUIDE
## TO A COMMON GOAL

*Clay B. Mansfield*
*Timothy W. Cunningham*
*with contributions from*
*Richard C. Harris*

**BUSINESS ONE IRWIN**
Homewood, Illinois 60430

Project editor: Margaret Haywood
Production manager: Ann Cassady
Art coordinator: Mark Malloy
Artist: Caliber
Compositor: Precision Typographers
Typeface: 11/13 Times Roman
Printer: The Book Press, Inc.

**Library of Congress Cataloging-in-Publication Data**

Mansfield, Clay B.
    Pension funds : a commonsense guide to a common goal / by Clay B.
Mansfield and Timothy W. Cunningham : with contributions from
Richard C. Harris.
      p.    cm.
    ISBN 1-55623-810-X
    1. Pension trusts.  2. Pension trusts—Investments.
I. Cunningham, Timothy W.  II. Harris, Richard C.  III. Title.
HD7105.4.M3  1993
332.6'7254—dc20                       92–12182

*Printed in the United States of America*
1  2  3  4  5  6  7  8  9  0  BP  9  8  7  6  5  4  3  2

# ABOUT THE AUTHORS

*Clay B. Mansfield* is the former chief investment officer of the $24 billion Pennsylvania Public School Employes' Retirement System. He was the creator and architect of the system's strategic plan, which identified and characterized the system's emerging pension liabilities, and set forth methods for meeting those liabilities. In accordance with the strategic plan, Mr. Mansfield also managed an in-house, fixed-income portfolio of almost $1 billion. He is president of Mansfield Investment Advisors, Inc., an independent institutional advisory firm dedicated to stewardship with almost $2 billion under advisement. Mr. Mansfield is also a principal in the investment firm of Benson, White & Company, which provides Master Money Management$^{SM}$, a fully integrated asset-liability money management service for institutional investors. Mr. Mansfield is the publisher of *The Trustee's Journal*, a periodical dedicated to helping pension fund board and staff members successfully discharge their primary obligation to pay pension benefits. He is a graduate of Bucknell University.

*Timothy W. Cunningham* is president of Springhouse Associates, Inc., an institutional investment consultant with $400 million under advisement. Mr. Cunningham is also a principal in the firm of Benson, White & Company and is editor in chief of *The Trustee's Journal*. He is a graduate of Williams College and of the American Graduate School of International Management.

*Richard C. Harris* served as a board member on the board of the Pennsylvania Public School Employes' Retirement System for over 15 years, serving as the independently elected representative of Pennsylvania's school boards. For many years, he was chairman of the system's finance committee.

# FOREWORD

The private pension system in the United States is young, dating back less than 50 years. It was a time of growth and expansion after the Second World War and hopes and expectations were high. Fringe benefits were recognized as something we needed, most particularly after the uncertainty of the war years. The Internal Revenue Service encouraged the growth of private pension assets by making contributions tax deductible if the benefit structure of the plan was equitable among employees. Most were, and the institution of a pension program in corporations was a relatively easy matter.

It was an era that predated the acceleration of inflation. It was a simple matter to calculate a benefit based on a particular year's salary. These were known as career average plans. At the end of a career, each year's accumulation would be added up and paid out at retirement. Each year, most corporations purchased that benefit from an insurance company in the form of an annuity and a certificate was issued to each employee. It was a relatively neat package. You accrued the benefit each year and an annuity was purchased to be payable at a later date.

With rare exception, there was little or no unfunded liability and the asset allocation of funds had a fixed-income orientation. In effect, unfunded liabilities were brought to zero each year through the purchase of annuities, thereby causing corporations no apprehension about funding in the future.

Two things happened to change this arrangement. Inflation accelerated so that career average plans provided an inadequate benefit at retirement. At the same time, equity returns approximated 19 percent during the 1950s. With 19 percent returns, corporations saw a way to cut pension costs by being able to substantially reduce contributions.

In the early 1960s, so-called final pay plans came into being. Under this arrangement, benefits were to be calculated on the basis of a salary toward the end of a career, and uncertainty about inflation was transferred from the employee and placed squarely on corporate shoulders. In response, corporations moved increasingly into equities, and the performance race was on. There were occasional minor setbacks to this trend during downturns in the equity markets, but the movement to equities seemed relentless. Indeed, this movement seems inevitable in hindsight. It was reasoned that only by investing in equities could a plan sponsor generate the necessary returns to meet promised benefits. These benefits could be actuarially forecasted but were virtually impossible to estimate with accuracy. The only sensible course seemed to be to keep driving for rates of return that substantially exceeded the spread between the salary assumption and the actuarial valuation.

In the mid-1960s the consultants came into the picture, initially to measure investment performance. In the late 1960s the Bank Administration Institute ordained methods for the calculation of returns. Gradually, a religious cult formed around the Standard & Poor's (S&P) 500 and other indexes. Modern portfolio theory gained converts as pension funds struggled to manage their increasingly diversified portfolios. Monthly and quarterly performance comparison replaced real concern for asset coverage of liabilities. Soon, it became more important to outperform an index or your peer group than it was to cover pension liabilities.

Then, during the 1970s, the pension system was dealt two blows. The first blow came from lower-than-anticipated equity returns. The second blow came in the form of higher-than-anticipated inflation. The combination of these two factors put a lot of funds under water, where the assets were not then sufficient to meet the projected liabilities.

The decade of the 1980s bailed everyone out with equity returns of about $17\frac{1}{2}$ percent, allowing many pension funds to become comfortably funded. Nevertheless, it seems doubtful that equity returns during the 1990s will reach the levels experienced in the 1980s. If that's the case, funded levels and the ultimate safety of retiree benefits will again come under pressure. The difference between the 1970s and the 1990s is that today time and demographics are working against us. The impact of the baby-boom related retirements leaves the pension system with less of an investment horizon, making the situation riskier than ever.

It has been my conviction for some years that the federal government will take over the private pension system and work it in tandem with, or collapse it into, the social security system. This will happen only if the private system falters, a prospect that seems likelier now than it was in the past. Corporations have high investment return estimates in their actuarial valuations, and we are entering a decade where those returns will be very tough to attain. This problem will be most acute if pension liabilities are valued on a discounted basis using lower interest rates than we have seen for some years. Additionally, states and municipalities are going through very strained budget periods. If negotiated pension settlements outstrip the ability to fund those settlements, ultimately, a hue and cry will arise for again reconciling assets with liabilities. As a consequence, into the fray will come the federal government to take over the private system, and state governments to take over municipal systems. This seems all but inevitable unless we refocus our energies back to the beginnings of the pension system and spend 100 percent of our time worrying about how we can manage assets to cover pension liabilities.

Many will claim that the present approach to pension fund management is more advanced and sophisticated than ever. But, to me, it is not at all clear that we have changed our ways for the better. While I understand the obstacles involved in advocating a return to sanity in the pension fund world, it is my belief that this unusual book represents a positive step in that direction.

William J. Crerend
Chairman, Evaluation Associates, Incorporated

# ACKNOWLEDGMENTS

We would like to recognize a number of individuals who have had an influence on the thinking behind this book. Notable among them are certain members of the Pennsylvania Public School Employes' Retirement System Board, including Bernie Freitag, Al Fondy, Jacque Angle, Dennis Ciani, and Joe Oravitz, as well as retired board members James McCann and Paul Lawrence.

The executive director of the Pennsylvania system, Jim Perry, was helpful in many ways over the years in the development of the ideas presented in this book. We would also like to thank Veronica Thomas and Mike Grubic, both professional staff members at the Pennsylvania system, neither of whom understand how helpful they have been in their support of this effort.

Our thanks to Chuck D'Ambrosio, editor in chief of the *Financial Analysts Journal*, for seeing that our project had merit and for introducing us to Business One Irwin.

Among the various people who have helped us clarify our thoughts and stay on track are Bob VanPelt, John Chappalear, Al Basilicato, and Ben Shaver. B. B. Cohen also deserves a word of thanks for having been an invaluable mentor to Clay over the years. Readers who may have had the pleasure of doing real estate business with Clay may be interested to know that, at least in this respect, Clay was long ago "Cohenized." Special thanks also goes to Delancy Davis, who has been a valued and trusted friend through many trying times.

Also, we feel compelled to acknowledge our deep gratitude and debt to Carter for his indefatigable support of this effort, and naturally, to the Carpenter.

Clay would like to thank his mother, Gert, whose common sense remains at the core of the ideas presented in this work. Clay can still remember his mom whispering to him, "Son, if it don't make sense to you, just say no!" Special thanks go to Bill, Clay's brother, who has been on the sidelines cheering him on for many years. Thanks also go to the boys at the "Y" for their inspiration, including Mike Patton, Bob Lech, and Ray Fry. Finally, Clay would like to thank Ike for her unfailing love and support.

Tim would like to thank his wife, Ann, for her forbearance through the occasionally obsessive periods when helping to create this work. And his father, Jack, and his mother, Shirley, for their advice, support, and editorial suggestions.

A word on style: For simplicity, the "I" in the book is Clay, and the "we" is both of us. All generic male references are intended to refer to females as well, and vice versa.

Clay B. Mansfield
Timothy W. Cunningham

# CONTENTS

# INTRODUCTION

This book is directed to defined benefit pension fund board members and the staff who serve them. The purpose of this book is to demonstrate to pension fund board members and fiduciaries that the "mysteries" of financial management are not mysteries at all, but can be understood by any intelligent person who serves a pension fund.

Our big-picture approach to pension fund management is unusual in today's world of specialized pension fund professionals. Whereas today's professionals concentrate on modest incremental improvements in investment results, we advocate an entirely different way of viewing pension funds. Put simply, our view is that pension funds exist to pay pensions at the lowest cost to contributors and the lowest risk of nonpayment of benefits to the plan participants.

The task of the pension fund fiduciary has no prescribed set of rules beyond the dictates of the law. These dictates are not prescriptive in nature, which is typical in situations that require common sense and good judgment. There is no blueprint of what to do and how to do it. The authors offer no easy or pat answers to the challenge of stewardship. But they do hope to help light the path with sound principles that will guide the common sense of pension fund fiduciaries as they discharge their responsibilities.

Unfortunately, common sense has often been the victim in a world that seems to place a premium on complexity. For all of us who are in the position of dealing with what seem to be complicated issues, sometimes it is helpful to stand back and ask: What should I be doing? What is the objective to be served? Much of the pension fund world seems single-mindedly focused on trying to beat the market. Assets are invested without regard to liabilities. Risks are taken without regard for consequences. This book tries to tackle these questions with straightforward common sense and sometimes anecdotes that help drive the point home. The following story illustrates what could happen if pension fund boards do not once again consider the safety of the pension fund first.

## ONCE UPON A TIME

At some point in the past, almost all pension fund boards attempted to practice the art of stewardship while managing other people's property. They knew they had to meet certain obligations, and they acted accordingly.

One day, after many years of labor, an obscure academic from a great university brought forth new and fascinating theoretical tools for the good board members to use in the discharge of their obligations. The academic wrote and preached tirelessly on the use—and the advantages—of these fine theories. Because of the prestige of the academic institution, and because of their fascinating complexity, a whole tribe of advisors was initiated into the use of these ideas. They went forth to tell pension fund board members about the new discovery. The advisors called themselves consultants and set themselves up as the priests of the new religion they called *modern portfolio theory*. Of course, everyone knew it was the Truth, but, to retain the presumption of humility, it was dubbed a theory nonetheless.

Now the board members were, for the most part, intelligent people who had undertaken a thankless obligation to others. They weren't so sure they *believed* in modern portfolio theory, but they knew that they should listen carefully. After all, the consultants and the university professors dealt with high finance and complicated algorithms (and who were the pension fund board members to question an algorithm anyway?). Besides, weren't stewardship tasks, such as paying pensions, boring and old fashioned at heart? The board members knew they had to enter the modern world, and what could be more modern than modern portfolio theory?

Gradually, little by little, the pension fund board members' sense of stewardship was dulled by the ceaseless incantations of the modern portfolio theorists who spoke of covariance, standard deviations, non-linear vector analysis, convexity, efficient frontiers, amplified alphas, and other equally "important" concepts. It seemed obvious to the modern portfolio theorists that cash would pour into the pension funds forever. Board members didn't have to worry about paying the pensions because, according to the modern portfolio theorists, pension funds were the *ultimate long-term investors*. After all, they said, wouldn't the pension funds be in business forever?

But demographics told another story. Due to prior increases in population, there was an impending flood of pension benefits that had to be paid with accumulated pension assets. These demographic realities implied that pension funds were short-term investors for today's obligations, medium-term investors for the next few years' obligations, and longer-term investors for obligations stretching out into the future. But nobody seemed concerned about when the bills would come due. Nobody was worried about stewardship anymore. The implicit danger of not preparing to pay nearer-term obligations didn't seem to concern the modern portfolio theorists.

A few board members weren't so comfortable with all this. Their intuition told them that huge numbers of people were going to retire in the shorter term, that these bills were approaching quickly, and unless they were careful, there would not be enough cash available to pay all the pensions as they fell due. These few pension fund board members knew that it would be unfair to future generations not to prepare carefully today to meet tomorrow's obligations.

But nobody was listening. These few board members were thought to be hopelessly out of touch with the latest advances in high finance. They were like cars with flat tires trying to travel in the fast lane of modern progress. These few pension fund board members, who simply wanted to make sure the pensions were able to be paid, were considered poorly informed dullards who were missing the new and exciting world of higher and higher investment returns that were there for the taking. Not to take advantage of these high returns was simply leaving money on the table, wasn't it? And, after all, these were risk-adjusted returns, and, you can't get hurt when all your returns are adjusted for risk, can you?

Then one day, after many years of worshiping modern portfolio theory, something interesting happened. Increasing numbers of people began to reach retirement age. It started slowly and gradually built up steam, until individuals began to retire in huge numbers. Every time you turned around, people were filling out papers and demanding that their pensions be paid. Additionally, an enormous number of people were on the verge of retiring, and they, too, would soon be clamoring for their pensions. And, imagine this: Every month for the rest of their lives, all these retiring people wanted their pension benefits to be paid in cash.

Board members across the land met in their conclaves as the torrent of retiring people gathered momentum. The pension fund board members had been told not to be concerned; the value of their assets was enough to pay the pensions. The modern portfolio theorists had assured them the probabilities would almost certainly be favorable over time, and not to worry. But the board members were worried because the capital markets were filled with great uncertainty, and time was running out before a veritable flood of pension promises fell due—promises that would have to be paid for many years to come. What were the board members to do now? Had they waited too long to focus on the issue of paying the pensions?

## MORAL TO THE PENSION FUND STORY

It seems appropriate to begin by summarizing the major points to be demonstrated in this book. While it may seem a little foolish, consider how a teacher organized a series of skits put on by a class of first grade children. These skits were centered around Aesop's Fables, and each fable was acted out by two or three children in appropriate costume. After each skit, the entire first grade class stood up and spoke loudly, and in unison, the word, *moral*. Then, together, all the kids would recite the moral of the preceding story, such as: Slow and steady wins many a race.

Now, during this entire production, the teacher was sitting down in front of the class, prompting the kids if they forgot a line. But the interesting thing was that the teacher didn't have to prompt any of the kids to speak in unison with the group when the moral of the story was recited. Each kid knew that his or her voice was but one of many, and if one kid didn't quite get all the words right, it really didn't matter, because no one would be singled out for embarrassment.

The purpose of verbalizing the moral after each story was to help the kids understand what the lesson was in every skit. By having them repeat the morals in unison, the teacher was probably trying to impress each lesson on the subconscious of her students.

There is both a child and a teacher in all of us. When it comes to learning new things, we are all a little like first graders. We need repetition. We don't want to be embarrassed because we don't know something. Sometimes we need prompting to get it right. The material in this book will be new for many readers. Forgive us for thinking it, but there are times when all of us could learn from first grade teachers. So, at the risk of alienating our audience, the following is a partial list of a few of the more important morals to our story.

- Pension funds exist to pay pensions at the lowest cost to the contributors and at the lowest risk of nonpayment of pension benefits to the plan participants.

- If we don't know where we are supposed to go, it's pretty hard to get there, and even harder to know where we are in the journey. Therefore, pension fund investment activities must follow a plan to pay pensions at the lowest cost to the contributors and at the lowest risk of nonpayment of pension benefits to the plan participants.

- Pension fund performance measurement consists of measuring how well a pension fund is progressing in its effort to pay and prepare to pay all the pensions at the lowest cost to the contributors and at the lowest risk of nonpayment of pension benefits to the plan participants.

- Modern portfolio theory is a tool, and must not be mistaken for a true financial objective. Paying pensions is a financial objective. Tools like modern portfolio theory are used to help us reach our objectives.

- A pension fund is not merely a long-term investor. Instead, it is a long term, a medium-term, and a short-term investor all at the same time. A pension fund's numerous investment horizons depend on the size and timing of its benefit payments to plan participants.

- Risk is meaningless unless we know what the consequence of possible losses will be. For a defined benefit pension fund, risk involves those decisions that result in a diminished capacity to pay all pensions, present and future.

- Pension fund board members must work courageously in the highest and best interest of the plan participants. They must not be complacent or agreeable for the sake of agreeing.

- Deliberate patience is required to avoid hasty action. If fewer actions are more carefully planned and executed, fewer mistakes are made. Don't underestimate the power of patient compounding.

- Understanding can only be found through common sense and simplicity. Don't be bamboozled by the experts who purport to have new and complicated ways to increase returns by a few basis points while disregarding common sense.

In addressing itself primarily to pension fund board members, this book is intended to fill a void. Pension fund board members have few choices when it comes to commonsense sources of advice.

Perhaps this book will serve as a chart and a sextant for board members as they seek guidance about where their pension fund must go. Common sense is a powerful compass that can be relied on heavily. This compass is available to you, too. Make frequent use of it and rely on it, because common sense gives direction to judgment.

Our fondest hope is that this little book will help lay pension fund board members understand and act on their responsibilities. It is intended to be sort of a ship captain's book for pension fund board members. Every ship must have a captain who has charts, a sextant, and a compass to make for a successful voyage. This pension fund business is not as complicated as it is made out to be. If we can make sense out of this business, we know you can too.

# CHAPTER 1

---

# THE PLAYERS

---

## PENSION FUND PEOPLE

Pension funds involve a wide variety of people. There are those individuals and organizations who contribute money into the fund. There are those who receive a pension today and expect to continue to receive a pension. There are those who do not yet receive a pension, but expect to when they retire. There are the service professionals who include staff members of the fund itself, as well as outside advisors, consultants, actuaries, asset managers, accountants, and attorneys. And there is the pension fund governing authority, usually a group of people who make up a pension fund board.

Essentially, four major groups are involved with most defined benefit pension plans: the members of the plan (both active and retired), the sponsoring organization (or organizations), those who serve in various support functions, and the governing board.

However, despite the many people involved, at heart, pension funds are about people who depend on their pensions. When those in the pension fund industry speak of the client, or the customer, they mistake either the plan, or those who serve the plan, as the customer. Notwithstanding this confusion, whatever concept one might have about pension funds must not be allowed to be divorced from the individual people who can lay claim to pieces of it, and who will come to rely on pension benefits to pay for basic necessities in their old age.

Pension funds are sponsored as deferred compensation plans by many different types of organizations, both public and private. While each pension fund operates differently, private pension funds are regulated by the federal government, whereas public funds are not.

Regardless of whether a fund is public or private, in most cases each pension fund is governed by a group of people who have the final say in matters of pension fund management. This group is the pension fund board. Pension fund board member judgments and decisions must be made with the objective of enhancing the plan's ability to pay all the pensions at the lowest cost to the contributors and the lowest risk of nonpayment of pension benefit to the plan participants. As a condition of their service, pension fund board members agree to be held accountable for their actions or failure to act. Importantly, pension fund board members are stewards of other people's money, and must act accordingly. Board members must not be afraid to stand up and do what is in the best interests of the members of the system.

Pension funds are served by a wide variety of professional advisors. Each pension fund professional should serve a different purpose in helping the fund achieve its overall objective of paying and preparing to pay all pension benefits at the lowest cost to the contributors and the lowest risk of nonpayment of pension benefits to the plan participants. All too often, however, pension fund professionals are not sufficiently aware of how their activities fit into the overall scheme of things. Neither is it always clear whether the professionals tell the board what to do, or whether the board tells the professionals what to do. Nonetheless, professionals have a responsibility to communicate what they know in an understandable way to the board, and the board must then decide what to do.

The strategies and actions of many of the professionals involved with pension funds ought to be coordinated by the pension fund board, but this rarely occurs in practice. The board hears from the actuaries about liabilities, and the board hears from consultants and money managers about assets, but rarely are both sides of the balance sheet approached in a unified manner. This is true even though the very purpose of the pension fund consists of the effort to integrate the liabilities to be paid with the assets needed to pay them.

Let's look a little more carefully at some of the major participants in pension funds.

## THE REAL PENSION FUND CUSTOMERS

It was the first week of November 1987. The financial world was digging out from the October 1987 crash. I was doing my own share of digging. If you will recall, the Dow Jones Industrial Average plunged 22.6 percent in a single day. This far surpassed the intensity of the 1929 crash. Nobody knew what would come next, least of all me. But not knowing didn't stop alarmists from predicting dark days ahead.

On this day in November, my private line rang in my office at the Pennsylvania Public School Employes' Retirement System. When I picked it up, Dennis Ciani, a board member, told me of his deep concern about the stock market crash. He went on to explain that the teachers he represented were also profoundly disturbed. To allay their concerns about the financial health of their pension fund, Dennis wanted to know if I would be willing to address the retirement and benefits committee of the teachers' union. I agreed immediately, and a date was set.

One week later, I went to a large hotel meeting room to speak to the committee members. As I entered the room, I was struck by the uniformly anxious look on the faces of the 22 teachers who had come to hear me. They were worried and looking to me for answers. Shortly after we sat down, the committee chairman introduced Dennis as one of the teacher representatives on the pension fund board. After Dennis made a few short remarks, he introduced me by stating I was there to answer any questions they might have about their pensions.

I remember the scene vividly. The chairman of the committee started things off with a simple bombshell: "Clay, how much money did we lose?" Everyone had the same worry: Was I sure the system was sound and could continue to pay pensions to the teachers? Then something happened that touched me deeply, and opened a door for me to see a new way of looking at the mission of our pension fund.

I was sitting in the front of the large conference table. To my right was a middle-aged woman teacher. As I was finishing, she leaned over to me and put her left hand on my right arm to get my attention. As I turned toward her, she had a troubled but trusting expression as she asked me, "Clay, are we OK?" I was almost moved to tears, for her question shook me right to my very core.

At that moment, reality came crashing in on me. Pensions are not just numbers; pensions are people, flesh and blood people. It seems so obvious, but many have forgotten. Maybe they never even knew. Pension funds are about the people who constitute their membership. They are not about stocks and fixed-income securities. They are not about managers, consultants, administrators, or bureaucrats. They are about people. In the pension fund world, the members of the pension fund are the final customers.

For those who work with pension funds, it is sometimes difficult to remember that pension fund customers come in all ages. Some of these people are young workers, just beginning their careers, whose pensions won't be paid for many years. Some are middle aged, closer to retirement than the younger worker, but not yet making claims on the pension fund for benefits. And some are older people, either retired or about to retire. These folks depend on their pension benefits, both in the near term and for the rest of their lives. On one end of the spectrum, then, younger plan participants have long-term investment needs, while older people on the other end of the spectrum have more immediate requirements.

Today, all those who serve the pension fund industry have mistaken either the plan, the board, the executive director, or the chief investment officer as the customer. This idea could not be farther from the truth. We must stop looking at the plan or its aggregated dollars as the true customer. In reality, these pension funds are more than a collection of assets. They are the future means of support for individual human beings. Pensions are a way people put off today's income to save for the future. Pension benefits provide the means for older individuals to pay for food, housing, and clothing. The investment community should realize that these people are their actual customers. They are not wealthy. They come in all ages. They don't have unlimited resources or infinite investment horizons. Neither can we assume they have any "excess" money to risk on speculative investments. Put another way, if we take $16 billion and divide it by 300,000 people, we find that each account is worth, on average, only $53,333. That's not a lot of money.

Even though there are obvious advantages to pooling money into a pension fund, the message is clear. To all those involved in serving pension funds, please understand who the real customer is, and don't be so cavalier in risking their retirement money.

## THE SPONSORING ORGANIZATION

Private pension funds are sponsored by various private entities, principally corporations. They serve as a form of deferred employee compensation. Defined benefit plans have a contractual obligation to pay pension benefits when those benefit payments fall due. The corporation must pay its share of the pension fund contributions out of corporate resources. These plans are highly regulated by the Department of Labor of the federal government in accordance with a complex body of law, regulation, and precedent. The most important of the pension fund laws are embodied in the Employee

Retirement and Income Security Act of 1974, known as ERISA. ERISA established rules to make sure that private defined benefit pension funds were funded properly and managed prudently. The ERISA laws and regulations, together with the applicable federal tax laws and regulations, govern most of what the private sector can and cannot do with its pension funds. ERISA also created a government-sponsored insurance program known as the Pension Benefit Guaranty Corporation (PBGC) for the private sector pension funds.

The PBGC was structured much like the Federal Deposit Insurance Corporation, whereby employers that operate pension funds pay a premium for the PBGC insurance. This premium has risen from its initial level of $1 per participant per year up to an average of about $23 per participant for 1991. Underfunded plans must pay more than overfunded plans, with a maximum 1991 premium of $72 per year per participant. Nevertheless, the present value of the probable PBGC liabilities far exceeds its capacity to pay those liabilities. Indeed, some analysts have estimated that the true cost of a premium for a seriously underfunded plan should be more than $4,000 per participant per year. Without drastic restructuring, this federal insurance program will prove to be costly over time. Accordingly, the ultimate safety of the core benefits and the probability of any increases in those benefits depend on prudent management of the pension assets, and on the viability of the sponsoring organization itself. For, even though government insurance is available through the PBGC, the viability of the private pension fund system depends on the health of corporate America and the prudence of its pension fund management practices.

In many corporations today, the defined benefit pension fund is structured and managed as merely one more facet of a corporation's overall financial picture. In this context, the impact of events involving the pension fund is viewed mostly in relation to how those events will affect the overall financial condition of the sponsoring company. Naturally, corporations seek to reduce contributions and smooth out fluctuations in earnings that might result from pension-related events. Regardless of intent, however, private pension funds are funded and operated in accordance with a uniform set of regulatory requirements.

In the public sector, pension funds are sponsored by a wide variety of governmental entities. As in the private sector, pension benefits serve as a form of deferred employee compensation. However, unlike the private sector, the taxpaying base of the governmental entity that serves as the plan sponsor serves as the source of contributions. In public pension funds, matters of politics and public policy often play an implicit as well as an explicit role in funding and management decisions. The health of the public pension fund is dependent on the prudence of the pension board as well as the willingness of taxpayers to support contributions into the fund. Public pension plans are not subject to the ERISA regulations and are not guaranteed by the PBGC. Instead, they are governed by a myriad of laws, regulations, and precedents promulgated by each sponsoring governmental jurisdiction.

## THE PENSION FUND BOARD AND ITS RESPONSIBILITIES

Throughout this book, we use the term *pension fund board*. Before proceeding any farther, let's examine what is meant by this phrase. In essence, a pension fund board is the term used for the governing body of a pension fund. Each pension fund has a slightly different makeup to its governing body, but generally a pension fund board consists of a group of individuals who have been entrusted with the management of the affairs of the fund on behalf of the beneficiaries. Some pension funds have different labels for their governing body such as board of trustees, pension committee, retirement committee, retirement council, or retirement board. Other pension funds have a single individual responsible for governing fund affairs. This person might be referred to as a *sole trustee*, or a *comptroller*. Regardless of the label, however, the function of the governing board or governing individual is the same. Please be aware, therefore, that this book is addressed to board members whether or not they may, in fact, be referred to as such by others. The board has certain powers and responsibilities, the basics of which are as follows:

- By means of their faithful service to the beneficiaries of the plan, pension fund board members are granted authority to act in the best interests of those beneficiaries.
- The pension fund board has the final say in most areas of pension fund management, and must be willing to assert that authority when necessary. The board alone serves as the representative of the members of the plan, and others must not be permitted to usurp the board's leadership role.
- The board must coordinate all the other players in the drama surrounding a pension fund. The board alone must establish policy,

direct action, monitor performance, and take corrective measures. In short, the board is responsible for managing the affairs of the pension plan to make sure that all pension benefits will be paid in full and on time. Perhaps the operation of a pension fund board can be better understood by likening it to the composer of a symphony who also conducts the orchestra. Without the composer, there is no music to play, and without the conductor, there is no coordination among the musicians. A board's compositiona l task involves working with the actuary and other advisors to develop a dynamic plan to pay the pensions. A board's conducting job consists of providing the leadership to managers and staff members who must execute the plan. In the world of the symphony orchestra, if there is no composition or no conducting, there is no music. In the world of a pension fund, either the lack of a plan or the lack of execution will diminish the ability to pay pensions.

While many would contend that the role of a pension fund board member has become more difficult in recent years, the most demanding tests are yet to come. Future challenges will include a greater emphasis on the discharge of the very duties that constitute the reason for a pension fund's existence.

Over the last 50 years, board members have seen the capital markets grow in complexity and sophistication. Many pension fund board members who are not financial professionals have been thrust into the role of keeping up with these changes while trying to understand the evolving variety of investment products available to them. Pension fund board members are not alone in the types of choices they have to contend with in today's capital markets. Numerous savings and loan (S&L) industry executives have now come to regret that they were led down the garden path into speculative investments in their search for ever higher returns. Increasing numbers and varieties of similarly alluring and often complex financial products are being offered to board members.

Yet, amidst this trend, pension fund board members have been sheltered by the demographic circumstances of their pension funds from many of the truly difficult decisions. As long as pension funds have been more than able to meet pension benefit obligations from current contributions, portfolios of investments have continued to grow from this source of positive cash flow alone.

However, as the population ages, it seems improbable that this happy trend will continue. It is more likely that the adequacy of the accumulated assets to meet the requirements of an aging population will constitute a board member's most nettlesome prospective concern. Any shortfall will be exacerbated as the number of active plan participants generating contributions into the pension fund falls compared to the number of annuitants being paid benefits. This will mean that pension fund board members may be forced to try to increase contributions over a smaller number of active plan participants, or decrease benefit payments to an increasing number of annuitants, or both. As neither of these choices are likely to be easy to make, board members must make hard decisions today to avoid having to make even harder decisions tomorrow.

Since a pension fund board member is called upon to put the interests of the plan participants first, there are many situations that call for the board member to exercise courage. In the context of a board member, courage is having the strength of character required to act as a "majority of one" where a matter of principle is at stake. When board politics threaten the plan, a board member is called upon to place the interests of the beneficiaries first. This is far easier to put in writing than it is to carry out in practice. But courage is needed to do the right thing. When board members are tempted to place all their focus on the capital markets, it takes courage and vision to act in the best interests of the plan participants. Regardless of what is happening in the markets, pension fund board members must hold steadfastly to their deliberate objective of preparing to pay the pensions. When board members don't understand something, it takes courage to stand up and say, "I don't understand."

In short, board members need to act courageously to stay on the right track. What is that right track? Simply this: All judgments and decisions must be made with the objective of enhancing the plan's ability to pay all the pensions at the lowest cost to the contributors and the lowest risk of nonpayment of pension benefit to the plan participants. This balance must be struck properly, without favoring either present-day concerns about the cost of contributions, or future concerns about the safety and adequacy of future benefit payments.

Board members are held accountable for their actions, regardless of how much authority they delegate to others. While a board can delegate authority to others to make certain decisions on its behalf, accountability cannot be delegated. Pension fund board members agree to be held accountable for their actions or failure to act as a condition of service. This accountability cannot be evaded, ignored, or dismissed. Today's board members would do well to consider the important consequences of their failure to provide courageous leadership in the face of the upcoming challenge of paying pension benefits.

## TOWARD A DEFINITION OF PENSION BOARD STEWARDSHIP

The notion of stewardship is central to the proper functioning of a pension fund board. A board member has a special relationship of trust with the members of a pension system for whose benefit pension assets are managed. The essence of stewardship is found in striving to find the balance between current and future needs by and through financial understanding, judgment, and common sense. Here's a simple story that illustrates this concept:

A man had two sons and three walnuts. He wanted to divide the walnuts fairly between his progeny. The problem was that the father did not want to appear to favor either son, both of whom he loved dearly. After careful consideration, the father came up with a solution that expresses the essence of stewardship. First he gave each son a single walnut. Then he explained to his sons that the third walnut would be used for seed to grow a tree that would produce thousands of nuts for years to come.

Like the father in this story, a steward must seek and find a balance between the demands of today and those of tomorrow. Stewardship is the constant search for the center of gravity and truth in all situations of economic life. The steward knows that he must remain in command of money and not let money command him. He must have a firm and consistent vision of money's use, purpose, and applications. These elements of money management must be used to bring enrichment and value to people's lives. A steward's tools are common sense, knowledge, experience, humility, patience, and the fortitude to calmly stay the course in the face of adversity.

While stewardship is easy to talk about, it is difficult to practice, often requiring great moral courage. Being a faithful steward of other people's assets requires a constant affirmation of the need to do what is right. Properly expressed, a steward does what is right both by intention and by conscious act. In the pension fund world, what is right means doing what must be done to ensure that all pension obligations are paid without fail at the lowest cost. There are many illustrations of the capacity people have to do what is right. Consider the following example of unusual moral courage:

The Civil War had been over for a number of years. In a small southern Virginia town, on a typical Sunday, the townspeople gathered to witness and share their belief. For the most part, few people in this all-white congregation stood out except for a noble-looking southern gentleman with a full white beard who sat quietly in a back pew. On this particular Sunday, he would be called upon to discharge his compassionate duty.

Midway through the Sunday service, a dignified, poor black man appeared at the main entrance to the church. Without hesitation, called by faith, and apparently unaware of the all-white assembly, the black man walked down the center aisle of the sanctuary. As he proceeded, the whispers began, not subsiding until he reached the altar, where he knelt in prayer. At that moment, there was an awkward and stunned silence. The congregation was confused, not knowing how to react, for this was the South—a South still emerging from the pain and loss of the Civil War.

And on this Sunday, the principles upon which that war was fought were quietly tested again.

Before the congregation could react, the dignified gentleman with the full white beard rose from his seat and moved toward the center aisle. All eyes were on him. He walked gracefully to the front of the church where he knelt next to the black man in silent prayer at the altar. The congregation, once confused, was now transfixed. They were witnessing an inspired act of grace and compassion. You see, the man with the full white beard who knelt in acknowledgment of the quiet need of expression of faith by the black man was none other than the epitome of the South, Robert E. Lee.[1]

Doing what is right amounts to recognizing the obvious and acting on it. The beauty of this story is that doing what is right doesn't require us to be a Robert E. Lee. We all have this power within us; we only need acknowledge our capacity, and then act on it.

## PROFESSIONALS WHO SERVE
## THE PENSION FUND INDUSTRY

For six years, while serving as the chief investment officer for a major public pension fund, I had an unusual porthole overlooking the professionals of the pension fund industry. These people included consultants, fixed-income managers, active equity managers, index fund managers, real

---

[1]Adapted from Billy Graham, "Points to Ponder," *Reader's Digest*, August 1958, p. 17.

estate managers, options managers, international managers, venture capitalists, actuaries, brokers, lawyers, custodians, and investment bankers. I'm sure I've missed a few, but you get the point.

These were, for the most part, consummate professionals. They had all their buzzwords and acronyms down pat. We've all heard these folks before. They say things like basis points, puts, repos, duration, convexity, time-weighted returns, syndicates, IRRs, MBOs, tranches, futures, spreads, and on and on. And, if this were not enough, they even had mystical phrases like clogging the equities of redemption, coherent bull markets, surplus space, and frozen initial liability. Webster would have loved these guys; he could have written a new dictionary once a year.

Professionals use this language to help them talk about and solve their problems. But what is the proper role of a professional who serves a pension fund? And how should a professional go about fulfilling that role? To answer these questions, we must first put things into their proper order and perspective.

Due to the complexities of various professional roles, it is not always clear whether the professional should be telling the board members what to do or the other way around. Accordingly, pension fund board members are sometimes uncertain about what it is their professionals should do. Each professional has been hired to perform a specific job. Together, these jobs must fit the overall needs of the pension fund as defined and directed by the pension fund board. A manager is hired to manage assets. An actuary is hired to assess liabilities and cash flows and make recommendations about plan funding. Various consultants are hired for their independent third-party expertise. Lawyers are hired to advise the board members on legal matters. By discharging their specific task, each professional helps advance the overall objective of the pension fund itself. The design and execution of that objective is the responsibility of the pension fund board, but every professional has a part to play.

Pension fund professionals should also understand their roles in the context of the larger picture. They do not need to know every detail of that larger picture, but should know how their efforts will benefit the pension fund. Professionals should seek innovative ways to help the pension fund attain its objectives.

Today, virtually all pension fund professionals are what might be called "incrementalists." They are busy squeezing out a few basis points one way or the other by using a common conventional blueprint for action. This blueprint has been based on statistics driven by the precepts of modern portfolio theory, and has come to dominate the investment practices of the pension fund industry. It is up to all those who render professional services to pension funds to continually reexamine their preconceived notions about what they should be doing, and not merely to follow blindly those who have gone before them.

While not every pension fund professional can live up to the description given above, one requirement for professional behavior must be paramount: Pension fund professionals must be able to communicate what they know in an understandable way to pension fund board members who can then use that information to further the objectives of the fund.

My mother was a wise woman who long ago drummed into my head the following piece of ham and eggs wisdom: "If a man comes to you hungry, and you feed him a fish, you have fed him for a day, and the man's condition remains unchanged. But if you take this same man, feed him, and then teach him how to fish, you have fed him for a lifetime." In teaching the man to fish, we change his life for the better, give him control over a measure of his destiny, and make our obligation to this man complete. Compassion cannot stand alone to effect change. Instead, it must have direction and understanding so a man will gain control over his life and actions. As a young pup, the message of this was hidden from me until years of life passed and I had gained experience and perspective.

Chief among the advice-givers are the consultants. These are the dispensers of Wall Street's and academia's current thinking. It is their accepted responsibility to investigate and integrate today's best investment ideas to the plan sponsor's highest advantage. Unfortunately, many of today's consultants offer a "fish of the day" to the plan sponsor. Whatever the financial community is pushing that month is offered up to the client. The hunger of the plan sponsor is dealt with only temporarily, because the advice-giver doesn't really understand the true needs of the pension fund. Put simply, that need is to be able to pay all of the pension obligations as they fall due. The real issues center around how pension assets must be managed and measured to meet those obligations, and not around the latest fad in finance.

In the time I spent as chief investment officer, no consultant ever inquired about the plan's economic liability, nor did any consultant analyze the demographic imperatives that ultimately determine the rates of return required to meet the system's financial obligations. To do so requires stewardship awareness. Instead, board members get advice of the day; one size fits all.

The resulting hunger for ideas is not satisfied—or dealt with beyond the moment. The only beneficiaries of this practice are the academics and the consultants themselves.

When, as pension fund board members, we shop for professional advice, we should pass over those who come to us with ready-made solutions. Instead, heed those who ask questions, who probe for fundamental problems, and who develop solutions that are clearly explained and connected to our overall charge of stewardship.

## SCHIZOPHRENIA IN PENSION FUND MANAGEMENT

Actuaries diagnose a pension fund's condition by calculating its liabilities. But it is investment managers who are hired to treat the condition, once it is diagnosed. Amazingly, the findings of the actuarial side of the pension fund world are almost never coordinated with the investment management side. A pension fund board is supposed to integrate the process, but rarely does it have the tools to do so. I am reminded of a story from my youth that illustrates the proper order of dealing with problems.

One day my older brother, William Henry, slammed the car door on my thumb. I was in great pain as my mom took me in to see Doc Wagner. The doctor's office on Main Street was across the street from Blinken's Funeral Home, a subtle reminder to get better, or else. Doc's waiting room was a converted porch. You know the type, with tables full of old magazines like *National Geographic, Boy's Life, Highlights for Children*, and *Reader's Digest*. A door led to his examination room, where the good doctor dispensed his medicinal and spiritual balms for his customers' ills.

I sat in the waiting room with my left hand wrapped around my right thumb, in a poor attempt to subdue the throbbing pain. When my time came, the door opened and Doc Wagner said "CB, I guess you're next; come on in and let's see what you've got." In the examination room, Doc told me to sit down, and then pulled up a chair to take a closer look at my wounded paw. While he was inspecting my thumb, I glanced around the room, which was well equipped with rubber gloves, tongue depressors, cotton swabs, and the usual medical paraphernalia.

"Hey Doc," I said, "What's the big deal? Can't you just patch me up and be done with it?" Then ol' Doc Wagner said something I'll never forget: "Be foolish to try to treat a patient without first diagnosing the problem, wouldn't it?"

Time passes, but principle never does. Doc Wagner was on to something. When he looked at a patient, he considered the situation carefully, diagnosed the condition, and then treated it. If it were only so easy for the board members of a defined benefit pension plan.

There is a marked lack of coordination between the diagnostic function and the therapeutic function of defined benefit pension fund management. This is as if Doc Wagner was responsible for diagnosing the patient, but neither treated the patient's condition nor communicated with the physician who did. In the chapters that follow, we will try to bridge the gap between these two intimately related sides of defined pension fund management. In so doing, we will attempt to place pension fund investing squarely where it belongs—in service of paying the pension liabilities as they fall due.

# CHAPTER 2

---

# THE RULES OF THE GAME

---

## THE DEFINED BENEFIT PENSION FUND

This chapter presents an unusual overview of the defined benefit pension fund. To understand and appreciate this view, we have to begin at the beginning and describe a few basic concepts because the fundamentals must be understood before the details can be dealt with.

Pension benefits can never equal more than the sum of contributions plus investment returns less expenses. Given this unalterable fact, a balance must be struck among the needs of today, the needs of tomorrow, and the ability and willingness of the plan sponsor to fund those needs appropriately. Increases in contributions cannot always be relied on to bail out a plan that falls short of the mark in paying and in preparing to pay all the pensions at the lowest cost and risk. Since contributions cannot always be relied upon and expenses are important but small in the grand scheme of things, investment returns become an indispensable part of funding pension benefits.

Maybe it should not have to be said, but a defined benefit pension plan exists to fund the defined benefit with cash. The capital markets offer an enormous variety of investment alternatives, all of which can be boiled down to two basic investment categories: ownership and debt. These categories are also called equities and fixed income, or simply stocks and bonds. Other investment alternatives are merely offshoots or derivatives of ownership and debt. In general, pension fund investment selections must trade off the need for conserving capital with the need for higher returns, all within the context of having enough cash to pay pension benefits when those benefits fall due.

We must understand how much must be earned on a defined benefit plan's assets to be able to pay the pension benefits when those obligations fall due. Yet paying pensions at the lowest possible cost involves assessing the risk of failure to do so.

Performance measurement can be a confusing topic. Consultants usually maintain that performance consists of the measurement of investment managers' returns relative to an index, or to a peer group. But performance measurement is only partially about these comparisons. Measurements that track a fund's ability to pay pensions are central to the purpose of the fund itself. The ability to pay pensions is determined by examining the relationships among a pension fund's assets, contributions, and liabilities. True pension fund performance measures how well a plan reduces its cost of funding, increases its funded ratio, and provides the liquidity necessary to actually make the benefit payments when due.

Measurement methodology is another confusing topic. It is related to the more general issue of the use of statistics and mathematics in pension fund management. Measurement techniques that are not relevant to the financial objectives of the pension fund are interesting, and even important, but less central than is commonly supposed.

Let's take these topics one by one and explore them a little more fully.

## WHAT IS A PENSION FUND?

Pension fund professionals live in a world of details. They analyze technical hedging strategies, balance portfolios using mathematical models, and read volumes of specialized research. Some limit their work to equities, others to fixed income, and still others labor in subdisciplines of these two. Board members of these funds get their share of the details as well. And so it is healthy to stand away from all the details and specialization to ask a fundamental question: What is a pension fund and how does it work?

This may seem like an easy question, but experience shows that some professionals are very specialized and have trouble answering clearly. Many newly appointed pension fund board members have trouble with this question as well, simply because it has never been explained to them. Those in the pension business, such as a manager, consultant, or board member, who cannot explain the workings of a fund to an intelligent but uninformed person may not have a firm grasp of the idea themselves. And if we fail to grasp the fundamentals, we fail to understand the mission of the fund.

**FIGURE 2–1**
**A Fully Funded Pension Fund**

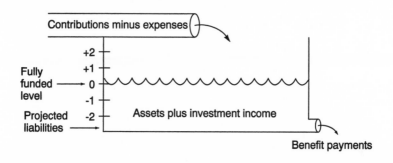

A pension fund is a system for the collection and disbursement of money. It is a little money factory that collects money in the form of contributions and adds it to its present financial assets. Of these, it pays out some as benefits to current beneficiaries, uses a small portion to cover expenses of the fund, and invests the rest for future disbursements. Represented algebraically:

Benefit payments = (Contributions − Expenses) + (Investment income)

It helps to look at a pension fund as a water tank holding pension assets. The tank is filled from two sources. The first source is the inflow of net contributions (i.e., contributions minus all fund expenses). The other source of growth in pension assets comes from investment income earned on those assets over time. The tank has a drain on one side that represents current and future pension benefit payments. On the other side of the tank is a scale to measure these obligations.

## THE FULLY FUNDED PENSION PLAN

When a pension fund's assets plus investment income and contributions minus expenses are calculated to be sufficient to meet the present value of its projected liabilities, the fund is said to be fully funded. It is said to have a funded ratio of 100 percent. That is, the pension fund has 100 percent of the assets needed to pay the present value of projected liabilities. This condition is shown in Figure 2–1.

**FIGURE 2–2**
**An Underfunded Pension Fund**

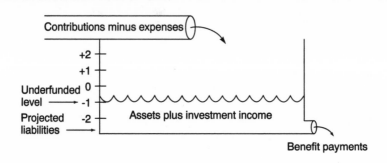

## THE UNDERFUNDED PENSION PLAN

When a pension fund's assets plus investment income and contributions minus expenses are calculated to be insufficient to meet the present value of its projected liabilities, the fund is said to be underfunded. That is, the pension fund has less than 100 percent of the assets needed to pay the present value of projected liabilities. The underfunded condition is shown in Figure 2–2.

If board members assume that the current beneficiaries' "drain" cannot (or should not) be reduced, there are only four ways to get the water level up in the years ahead:

1. Reduce the outflow of expenses.
2. Open up the spigot, increasing the inflow of contributions.
3. Make the current volume in the tank expand through investing.
4. A combination of all the above.

## THE OVERFUNDED PENSION PLAN

A third condition of a pension fund is to have assets plus investment income and contributions minus expenses that are more than sufficient to meet the present value of projected liabilities. In this event, a fund is said to be overfunded. That is, the pension fund has more than 100 percent of the assets needed to pay the present value of projected liabilities. Using the

**FIGURE 2–3**
**An Overfunded Pension Fund**

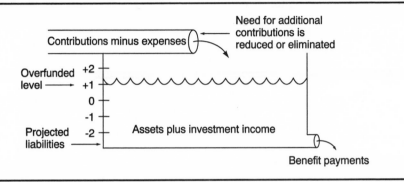

same type of tank analogy used before, the overfunded condition is shown in Figure 2–3.

## A DYNAMIC PENSION FUND MODEL

If benefits are expected to be at a certain level, then the extent to which board members can reduce expenses and assure investment income means fewer contributions will be required. Failure in that task makes greater contributions necessary. In Figure 2–4 our tank analogy is taken one step further, as we show the dynamic relationships among the elements of a pension fund. Now it looks a little like a toilet tank (no kidding). The float mechanism goes up as the level of assets and investment income goes up and drives down the need for contributions, represented as a valve governing the flow of net contributions into the system. Similarly, when the assets and investment income level is too low, contributions must be increased to pay the benefits when they fall due. If benefits are increased, or decreased, the volume draining out on the lower right will increase, or decrease, as shown by the valve on the outlet drain.

## ACTUARIAL ASSUMPTIONS

When actuaries make the calculations that determine the funded status of a pension fund, they estimate the value of certain variables. They look at

**FIGURE 2–4**
**A Dynamic Pension Fund Model**

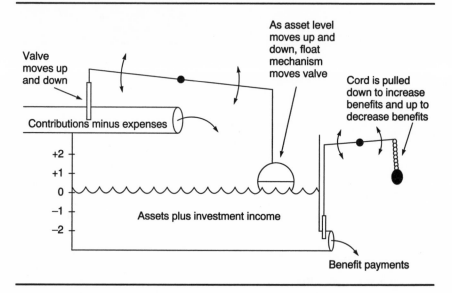

the demographics of the plan and its historic retirement and mortality patterns. These elements are usually fairly well established and don't tend to shift one way or the other.

Actuaries have to make other assumptions that are harder to nail down than demographics. Most vexing are the assumptions that have to do with future salary or benefit increases, as well as assumptions about future investment earnings and the discount rate, to arrive at the present value of pension fund liabilities. These calculations are particularly important because they form the basis for establishing the rate of contributions into the pension fund. If the calculations are based on unrealistic assumptions, the actuarial process becomes less helpful as a tool for the wise management of pension fund assets and obligations.

For example, if assumptions about salary increases are too low, or those about investment income too high, the pension fund will find itself having to raise future contributions to make up the difference, or eventually somebody's pension will either be cut, or not get paid at all. Alternatively, unrealistically high salary assumptions or unrealistically low investment income assumptions may force an unnecessarily high level of contributions into the fund.

As board members, we must not abandon the tedious process of actuarial analysis simply because those among us have honest disagreements about actuarial assumptions. Pension fund board members, in conjunction with their actuaries, must endeavor to come up with a reasonable set of assumptions in order to manage the pension fund to prepare to meet its obligations at the lowest cost and risk. To do otherwise is to avoid the hard job of stewardship.

## CONTRIBUTIONS INTO THE PENSION FUND

As we consider the options facing pension fund pension fund board members, there is one important caveat: In an abstract sense, we can simply make a statement that contributions will occasionally have to be increased. In the real world, though, the ability to increase contributions is severely constrained by a multitude of factors. Accordingly, because of their unyielding obligations, board members cannot rely on increases in contributions to fund pension benefits. This fact places a high premium on successful investing and efficient fund management.

A pension fund should not be a pay-as-you-go system. In a pay-as-you-go pension plan, current contributions are made for the benefit of current pension recipients. Instead, the intent should be for each generation of contributors to fund its own retirement without burdening the next generation. Many pension funds have a small number of current annuitants relative to future retirees, so the current inflows of cash often exceed the current outflows. Large contributions today are intended to support the even larger payouts due in future years. This is a great deal more sensible—and responsible—than the pay-as-you-go systems, which are destined to place the horrendous retirement burden for the large baby-boom generation upon the backs of the next, and much smaller, generation.

Unfortunately, it is not always possible to arrive at a fully funded status in public pension funds that must rely on the actions of politicians to fund contributions with taxes, and which have no clear and consistent mandate to strive for full funding. Especially with many larger public pension funds, while the objective of full funding is necessary and desirable, we may have to realize that, as with many human objectives, a fully funded status may not always be possible to attain. But this simple fact should not deter board members from the effort to achieve full funding any more than the fact of war deters men from pursuing peace. Without an ideal condition to strive for, the attainment of even more modest goals is much less likely to happen. In light of this reality, a sincere effort is necessary to do the best possible job.

## RISKS UNIQUE TO PENSION FUNDS

If this big-picture portrayal of the pension fund seems a bit neat and tidy, we should know that it is seldom thus. The world is an uncertain place, and the pension fund is subject to specific types of unforeseen outcomes. These risks come in three varieties:

1. *Owner risk*—This is the risk that the assets owned by a pension fund suffer losses, or that the pension fund suffers a lower overall rate of return than anticipated. A pension fund has, to use the words of Robert Frost, "promises to keep." Obligations to pension participants must be met, but there is always the risk that the return on invested assets will fall short of the level of return that was planned to pay benefits as they fall due.
2. *Funding risk*—The risk that, for whatever reason, insufficient contributions will be made to fully fund future benefits. In public pension plans, funding risk can relate heavily to the vagaries of the political process.
3. *Cash flow liability risk*—This is a first cousin to the banker's admonition to never borrow long to lend short. In the pension world, this translates into this dictum: Never invest solely for long term when the demographics of the fund are short term, medium term, and long term. If we do, cash obligations can force us to incur significant unrealized losses, triggering a painful rise in the level of required contributions.

All investors bear investment risks. In managing a pension fund, pension fund board members bear investment risks *plus* these three particular uncertainties. They make the task of a board member especially difficult and challenging.

## COLD, HARD CASH

The driving force behind a defined benefit pension fund is funding the defined benefit. How are benefits funded? With cash, naturally, even though many other facets of pension fund management are not calculated on a cash basis. As we will see later in this chapter, it is often helpful to establish the rate of return to get from a beginning value of pension fund assets to a required future level of pension asset values. This is a useful way of looking at the big picture of a pension fund's liabilities. It's a good way to boil down the ultimate task of becoming fully funded to a single set of measurements. And, while these measurements must be revised on a periodic basis, the laudable goal of becoming fully funded remains constant and necessary. Unfunded liabilities are like any debt; the principal must be retired through repayment. It's similar to a mortgage lender calculating mortgage payments so the borrower knows what he has to pay each month to retire his obligation to the bank. Yet, the homeowner has to find the cash to pay the mortgage every month and write his check to the bank to prevent foreclosure.

Board members are faced with a more difficult set of interrelated problems than the homeowner. A pension fund must seek to retire its unfunded liabilities *and* plan to pay its annuitants in cash. Pension fund board members must know how they are progressing in their effort to fully fund the pension benefits and have a simple benchmark to measure progress toward this goal. But since only cash pays the pensions, it is absolutely imperative for board members to have a cash plan to be able to assure the pension payments will actually be made.

We can calculate the present value of today's assets and then determine the future value needed tomorrow to fund pension liabilities. We can then discount that future value of the liabilities back to the present to see where we stand today. And, as any actuary will tell us, depending on our discount assumptions, the present value of our liabilities can be manipulated easily. Yet, while the present value of both the defined benefit pension assets and its liabilities changes from day to day, the minimum future value of those liabilities remains relatively inflexible. What's more, while the present values of assets and liabilities go both up and down, future liability values usually go only up and not down. That is because future liabilities track pension benefits that are often virtually impossible to reduce and that can be increased from time to time when cost-of-living adjustments (COLAs) and other increased pension costs are applied retroactively across a plan.

More importantly, pension liabilities must be paid in cash, not in stock or real estate. For this reason, in a defined benefit fund, the requirement for cash is absolute. The benefits must be paid, and they must be paid on time and in cash. If we rely on asset sales to generate cash, those assets are worth only what somebody is willing to pay for them at the time we need to sell them. Cash payments of benefits are made at specific times to specific individuals. So the need for specific amounts of cash at specific points in time drives the entire system. And the need to have the cash on hand to pay all pension benefits when they fall due, come hell or high water, is what constitutes the most important and overriding objective of a pension fund.

Contributions provide cash flow, but it is the earnings on those contributions over time that give the ability to pay out more in benefits than the amount of contributions taken in. Yet, we cannot focus on an infinite period in order to plan our cash needs because benefit payments are made in finite dollars paid at finite intervals to real people. Instead, we have to focus on the cash needs over reasonable periods of time and update the assessment of those needs regularly. The question in funding benefits is this: As pension fund board members, how are we to plan our cash flows to be able to fund *all* pension benefits in a responsible, careful, and deliberate manner?

This means that when the pensions fall due, we have to be able to pay them. It also means that we have to plan for that eventuality by taking into account the inherent uncertainties in the world. We cannot assume that if we get into trouble we can sell off assets willy-nilly because we have to count on the earnings from *those* assets to pay future pensions. We cannot assume that a pension fund is forever, when the cash needs to pay the pensions are firmly tied to the liabilities and the changes in benefits in our specific plan. And we must admit that we are susceptible to the ups and downs in the value of our assets over the course of time.

Board members can use the statistical techniques in modern portfolio theory to help in the effort to plan for paying the pensions. These statistical techniques can be used to assure us that we have planned for the optimal exposure to any given long-term volatile asset class to be able to convert profits in those long-term assets into cash to pay the pensions.

Skeptics might say that if the stock market is in a down period when we need to raise some cash, we don't have to sell stocks into the bad market, we sell off some of our fixed-income securities, instead. On the face of it, in today's pension fund world, this seems to be a reasonable short-term solution. But that is just what it is, a short-term solution. If we sell our fixed-income securities to meet a cash crunch, then we lose the future income on those fixed-income securities, putting a crimp in future cash flows and also losing the compound income on the lost cash flows. This is a double whammy that alleviates today's pain by inflicting that pain on others tomorrow.

Others may say that contributions can always be increased to make any shortfall in cash. But we cannot responsibly count on contributions being increased on demand to meet pension benefit payments. Even given the ability of many public pension systems to mandate tax increases to pay pensions, there is no way to sugarcoat the reality that the political process will not tolerate these tax increases indiscriminately. Responsible pension fund board members will probably agree that it is unwise to bet peoples' pensions on the ability to increase contributions at will.

The only controllable alternative is to plan well in advance to meet cash needs. Board members can accomplish the cash planning task through a number of relatively easy steps:

1. Select a planning horizon of a specific number of years into the future. This is similar to selection of the planning period for the hurdle-rate calculation. For ease of calculation and most effective use of board time, the cash planning period can be made identical to the hurdle-rate planning period.

2. Examine demographics and retirement patterns to understand the timing and size of emerging liabilities.

3. Project cash requirement levels for each year of the cash plan. It may be a good idea not to rely on contributions to meet your cash requirements. This assessment comes from the potential instability of contributions in the future. If, for any reason, contributions are not made in a timely fashion, there may not be enough cash in the plan to pay pensions without unexpectedly having to sell assets.

4. Examine any annual difference between the cash generation capability of your portfolio and the cash requirements in your plan.

5. The difference between liabilities and the plan cash generation is the cash requirement. It can be funded from income, capital gains, selling assets at or below cost, or increasing contributions. Plan a strategy to meet the cash requirement through one or more of these methods. A more detailed explanation of a carefully designed cash plan is presented in the chapter entitled "Pension Funds and Asset Allocation."

## THE CASH COVERAGE RATIO

The cash coverage ratio is a pension fund performance measurement tool that allows plan sponsors to understand how well they have planned their cash requirements. The cash coverage ratio is determined by holding funded ratio assumptions and contribution assumptions constant for the calculation period. Once these critical assumptions have been made and held constant, the cash coverage ratio is defined as the percentage of benefit payments that can be covered by cash and cash equivalents without causing a decline in either the funded ratio or an increase in contributions.

We must be careful to plan for emergencies. Almost all personal financial planners recommend that individuals maintain three to six months' worth of cash reserves to deal with unforeseen problems and guard against insolvency. A pension plan must also have an emergency cash plan to deal with the uncertainties in the world. Board members must remain vigilant about a pension fund's cash flow. Funding pension benefits is too important a task to have to face an emergency cash crisis without a realistic plan.

In the world of finance, coverage ratios serve as guidelines for prudent action. A lender, for example, always wants to see that the cash flow available for debt service is well above the debt service itself. While the various ratios differ in application, those that compare available cash to obligations to be paid with cash are always greater than one to one. That is, we must always strive to have more cash than the obligations to be paid with that cash. In many lending situations, cash coverage ratios are held to a minimum of 120 percent. This does not seem to be an imprudent minimum for a pension fund to strive for when planning its cash coverage. Therefore, when planning cash coverages, an appropriate target cash coverage ratio should always be greater than 100 percent, and possibly as high as 120 percent or more to allow for cash emergencies.

## KNOW THE STRIKE ZONE

There is a story about Ted Williams, the legendary baseball player. It applies to all of us who try to plot successful courses in life, and it revolves around a rare interview given to a press reporter. Here it is.

> Searching for the secret of Ted's hitting prowess, a reporter brought up the subject of Williams's vision, which was 20/10. Yes, Williams said, his eyes were better than average. What's more, Williams pointed out, he understood exactly where the strike zone was. That resulted in fewer strikes, more walks, but fewer hits. The sports reporter seized upon that statement and suggested the slugger could get more hits if he swung at some balls just

slightly out of the strike zone. Williams replied that he could get more hits; however, he made it a particular habit not to swing at pitches outside the strike zone. "Well," replied the dogged reporter, "why, if you could get more hits, don't you slightly alter your practice?" Williams responded, "Because doing so would mean there would be no place to draw the line." The interview concluded on that note.[1]

The meaning of that statement was lost on the sports reporter but shouldn't be lost on us. What was that message? Clarity of understanding comes from the practiced discipline of knowing the parameters within which we must operate effectively and with our greatest force of purpose. Without this discipline, we succumb to the seduction of things beyond the limits of our concentration. And that little reaching muddies our judgment enough that through this act, our ability to find, measure, and maintain success is dramatically reduced. What is the connection between this discussion and financial stewardship? Simply, stewardship is knowing the strike zone and judiciously making it work for us in managing financial affairs on behalf of others. In the world of pension stewardship, this means knowing what must be earned on the pension fund's assets to be able to pay the pension benefits when those obligations fall due.

But is it this simple? Yes and no. The legendary investor Warren Buffet was supposed to have said, "For me, investing is easy. It is like being a hitter in baseball where there is no umpire. All I have to do is wait out the pitcher of opportunity until that fat pitch comes along down the center of home plate. Then I cream it." But Mr. Buffet's analogy is inappropriate for pension fund board members. Unlike Mr. Buffet, board members must play the game with an umpire and an unyielding baseline of real obligations. This reality and these arbitrators significantly change the dynamics of play.

Imagine for the moment instead of Mr. Buffet we are the batter. There are three men on, no outs, bottom of the ninth, and behind by only one run. A new pitcher has been brought in and our batting coach has given us all his prior performance statistics. The new pitcher's style and record are known to us, and we have been coached to expect either a curve or a sinker. With no outs, we can afford to look them over. We step up to home plate. We first adjust ourselves to the batter's box. Then we check

---

[1]Richard Saul Wurman, *Information Anxiety* (New York: Doubleday, 1989).

out the umpire. He is an imposing figure, a performance consultant dressed in "index blue."

Before we can grasp the reality of the situation, the umpire barks, "Batter up!" Immediately, we turn and address the plate and the "pitcher" of market opportunities. We look at the umpire nervously. We forget about the needs of the plan participant. Well, never mind, the game's in front of us, isn't it? In any case, we take a firm grip on our "discipline" bat, get in our batter's crouch, and wait for the pitcher's first offering.

The pitcher rubs the ball, hoping to infuse it with some market magic to confuse us. He steps to the mound, immediately goes into his motion, and lets fly his first offering—a curve. We wait, measure the pitch's hitting potential, and decide to let it go by. The pitch is low and a little to the outside. But the umpire doesn't see it that way, yelling "Stee-rike one!"

"What . . . are you crazy?" we mumble as we look back at the umpire.

Unflinchingly, he responds, "Strike one!" Again, we get set in our batter's stance and the pitcher delivers his next pitch: a sinker, low and to the inside. We let it go by. But the umpire yells, "Stee-rike two."

"Aw, come on," we shout, but the umpire merely scowls.

Now, more determined than ever, we get set in the batter's box to face the next pitch. The pitch, the swing; it's a spit ball! We catch just a piece of it, and the ball is immediately caught by the first baseman; then it goes to second, and then third, and the game's over.

Get the picture?

For those who manage others' money and who are answerable to others, the answer to where the strike zone is, which pitches are fair game, and even what our hitting strategy should be are never as simple as they are for Mr. Buffet.

## DEFINE THE STRIKE ZONE

Simply put, for a defined benefit pension fund, the strike zone is the required rate of return on assets necessary to fully fund current and anticipated future pension obligations.

This definition implies that certain assumptions be made to develop a single targeted rate of return that a pension fund can use in planning to meet its obligations. Sometimes this required rate of return is referred to as the hurdle rate of return because it is the return that must be earned in order to jump over the obstacles to becoming fully funded. For an example of a hurdle-rate calculation actually employed by a major public pension fund, please refer to the appendix at the end of the book.

These comments about the strike zone are particularly important to those board members of underfunded defined benefit pension plans. The reason for this should be obvious. The underfunded plan is at the most risk of not being able to meet its obligations in a timely manner. While the challenges for an overfunded plan are no less real, the underfunded plans are the ones that have a greater need to make every at-bat count for a hit.

Nevertheless, board members of fully funded plans and overfunded plans must also remain vigilant. Their responsibilities include the endless task of assuring that their pension funds remain fully funded through all manner of changing circumstance. The overfunded plan cannot afford to relax because of the changing value of its assets and liabilities. So, regardless of the funding status of a pension plan, defining and hitting in the strike zone is important for all.

In every way possible, we must study the specific factors that together define the probable future liabilities of the fund. A board member's first and most important concern revolves around the demographics of his pension plan. That is, how many active and retired participants are involved, how old are they, and what do we know about their retirement patterns? We also need to know how the pension benefit obligations are calculated, and how those calculations are affected by changing circumstances such as salary or wage increases. We need to know what contribution levels are implicit in our assumptions, as well as the possibility of obtaining an increase in contributions should an investment program fall short of the mark. We must examine the consequences of any future changes in benefits due to external forces such as inflation or deflation.

In this analysis, one must guard against becoming overly optimistic or pessimistic about the future. The right balance is to err (or at least lean modestly) toward the conservative side in order to allow for life's inevitable surprises. This is especially important when board members consider the high price of failure to fund benefits when they fall due.

After probable liabilities have been outlined and caution has been taken to remain realistic and clearheaded about the assumptions used in planning for the future, the next critical element of the problem is to establish a hurdle-rate planning period. Many pension fund experts talk about how a pension fund is the ultimate "long-term investor." They're assuming that a pension fund needs no particular time horizon to determine its investment policy. Nothing is farther from the truth. In fact, pension fund investment horizons will tend to mirror the ages and tenure of the plan participants. When viewed in this light, the objective of full funding becomes much more important.

It is ironic that we have to deal with at least one fiction even if we have realistically appraised our liabilities and calculated our required rate of return. That fiction is the need for a hypothetical termination point to the pension plan. A finite termination point is selected as that point in time when we intend to reach a fully funded status. A specific point in time is selected because we can only deal rationally with the world's uncertainties by focusing on a finite period of time. As human beings, we cannot focus on an infinite horizon when dealing with finite decisions. This fact alone is justification enough to urge the selection of a finite planning period.

Nevertheless, there is an even more important motive to plan for a finite funding period because the the size and timing of pension liabilities tend to be uneven over time. If the liabilities were constant and the contributor to annuitant ratio was constant, a standard planning period would be right for every pension fund at all times. But the reality is not that simple. Liabilities change from plan to plan and within each plan over time. The right course for a pension fund with one set of liabilities to pay might be precisely wrong for a pension fund with a completely different set of liabilities to pay. What's more, the right planning period for a given time in an individual pension plan's history might be completely wrong at a different time. Therefore, a critical examination of emerging liability trends forces pension fund board members to select a more realistic finite planning period to prepare to pay pension benefits when they fall due.

Most pension funds need to think in longer time frames than a mere few years to plan adequately for the future. Yet, for a seriously under-funded pension fund to use a 30-year planning period to strive for full funding is unrealistic if there is a large increase in liabilities coming over the next 15 years. Similarly, if board members have large numbers of participants reaching retirement age within 10 years, it would be foolish to have a planning horizon of 20 years. So, we have to select a reasonable planning period relative to our ability to fund pension payments at the lowest possible cost and risk. Pension fund board members must make assumptions to plan, but those assumptions must be coupled with the reality of the liability stream to be effective. Board members have a critical need to focus their attention properly on the problems, challenges, and disciplines necessary to carry out a realistically conceived plan during a realistic period.

How do we choose a realistic planning period? We start by examining where we are today and where our emerging pension liabilities will put us in the future. Then we must select a planning period appropriate to the task of funding the liabilities as they change. In the United States, baby-boom demographics present a picture of dauntingly high increases in future pension liabilities. The liability-specific demographic circumstances of a given pension plan must drive the selection of a planning period.

As previously discussed, this entire process is not easy, given the controversial variables whose values must be assumed. Actuaries are familiar with the difficulty in agreeing on appropriate assumptions for the calculation of funded ratios and contributions. Yet board members, together with their actuaries, must not shy away from making reasonable sets of assumptions merely because it is hard and controversial work. Of particular importance to board members in certain public pension funds is the problem that statutory impositions of unrealistic actuarial methods may have to be ignored as the board plans its own strategy to pay the pensions.

Finally, in choosing a planning period board members must periodically reassess and recalculate the liabilities and thus the required rate of return. It is not a bad idea to revisit these issues once a year to update numbers and assumptions with whatever new information we have about current circumstances. In this way, while we select a specific planning period to define a strike zone, we retain the ability to react appropriately to the pension fund's needs on a timely and informed basis.

Once the emerging liabilities are defined and a planning horizon selected, the next step is the actual calculation of the required rate of return. This becomes a relatively easy task from an arithmetic perspective, once the critical assumptions have been agreed upon. A rather simplistic illustration is shown in Figure 2–5 to help us conceive of how a required rate of return looks in diagrammatic form.

Figure 2–5 is really not mysterious. The angle, or slope of the line, represents the required rate of return on assets as calculated in accordance with the assumptions determined by the specific circumstances surrounding a particular pension fund. We have referred to the slope of this line as the strike zone. This is the required level of return on pension fund assets to become fully funded by the end of our planning horizon.

**FIGURE 2-5**
**Determining a Required Rate of Return**

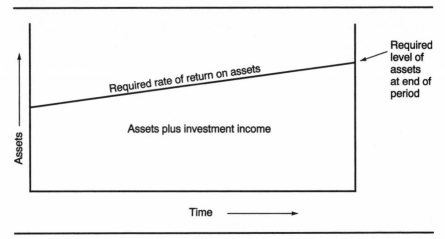

Required rate of return on assets

Required level of assets at end of period

Assets plus investment income

Assets

Time ────────▶

Some may say that the required rate of return is a meaningless number because it is based on easily changed actuarial assumptions based on balance sheet manipulations. The apparent malleability of funded status calculations may appear irrelevant when compared to the inflexible requirement of paying pension benefits in cash, on time, and without fail. Yet, in the effort to plan for the future properly, both cash flow requirements as well as balance sheet requirements must be considered fully. The required rate of return integrates balance sheet issues. If we do an inadequate job of balance sheet preparation, having the cash to pay all pensions, present and future, will be compromised. If the sole focus is on cash flow requirements over a given period, we never know whether we are impairing our ability to pay future pensions without resorting to big increases in contributions. And we must remember that contributions cannot easily be increased at will to cover shortfalls.

If a pension fund does not plan well, it may find itself faced with the task of selling off assets being held for future needs to pay today's pensions. If improperly managed, this practice merely shifts today's problem onto the backs of the next generation, who will then find themselves with fewer assets to pay for their own pensions. This is why we need to manage cash requirements as well as manage the funded status. Without knowing how a pension plan is doing relative to all of its obligations, one cannot plan responsibly to meet future cash flow needs.

A hurdle-rate calculation provides a critical tool in pension fund management. A pension plan must have the objective of attaining full funding within a finite time frame in order to plan prudently, realistically, and fairly for the future. This is true even though the job of calculating funded status can be built on shifting sands. A hurdle-rate target is important even if we never reach a fully funded status because it is important to know if we are making progress in preparing to meet future obligations. The hurdle rate of return boils down the complex and often confusing job of choosing among investment alternatives into a way to connect the asset side of a pension fund's balance sheet with its liability side.

A hurdle rate of return target integrates the actuarial job of calculating liabilities with the investment job of investing assets, thereby establishing a benchmark for pension fund board members to use as they strive to reach a fully funded status. As a benchmark, a hurdle rate is therefore a relatively simple way to help board members navigate through capital market alternatives within the context of a pension plan's unique circumstances.

Now that we have defined the strike zone, who is the umpire? Who decides what liabilities exist and what rates of return will be required on the pension fund assets? The answer is that only the pension fund board members can serve as the final arbiters of the pension fund's assumptions about the future. While a pension fund's actuary is counted on to calculate and define what the fund will need in order to meet all of its obligations to its beneficiaries, the final decision must remain with the board. Thus, together with the actuary, board members must agree on a uniform set of rules and a level playing field. And until the rules are based on the specific reality of a pension fund's liabilities, confusion will reign and the exercise of true stewardship is impossible.

## HIT IN THE STRIKE ZONE

Now that we have a good idea of what the strike zone is in pension fund investing, let's turn to the question of how to step up to the plate and consistently hit the ball within that strike zone. This is no easy task because every pension plan's situation is different. What is right for one plan may not be right for another.

Perhaps the most difficult task in this regard is to control our greed. Pension fund board members have a special obligation to be aware of their impulses to strive for ever greater returns. When this striving becomes unrealistic, it can feed an insidious emotion that taints the pursuit of meeting stewardship obligations in a responsible, careful, and deliberate manner. Without a clear sense of what is an appropriate level of risk, an insatiable appetite for ever higher returns is stimulated. What's more, because these impulses have no end point and no clear objective, we never know how much of a return is too much, or too little. Therefore, striving blindly for ever higher returns has no place in pension fund stewardship where the true objective is paying pensions.

While board members must be ever vigilant to the financial objective of paying all the pensions at the lowest cost and risk, money managers have a different charge. Money managers must serve the pension plan by providing whatever type of management they have been hired to provide. A money manager's objective is to hop on the treadmill and to run in the direction he has been ordered. Money managers must use every faculty at their disposal to carry out the orders of the board.

In a way that board members cannot, then, active money managers may be permitted to strive blindly for ever higher returns if they have been hired with that objective in mind. Yet money managers must also remember that the ultimate purpose of their activity is to fund pension benefits and thereby be more sensitive to the true needs of their clients. The reason that an unfettered pursuit of ever higher returns is inappropriate as the principal objective of a pension fund is that higher returns are inescapably connected with higher risks.


## RISKLESS RETURNS AND HURDLE-RATE RETURNS

Because risk and return are two subjects that receive much attention in the world of investment, let's examine how risk is connected to the hurdle rate of return.

In the jargon of what is known as modern portfolio theory, there is an important notion called a riskless return. A riskless return doesn't mean risk free; it just means obligations of the U.S. government. These securities do have risks associated with them, but because they are backed by the U.S. government, we agree that they are as risk free as possible. So, if board members want the safest rate of return, they can build a portfolio based solely on U.S. Treasuries.

The trouble with a riskless return is that it is so safe it doesn't have to be very high to attract investors. And, as the capital markets change over time, the riskless rate of return also changes. Even so, because of its safety, the riskless return serves as an important benchmark in our attempt to hit in the strike zone. That is, at any time, pension fund board members can always count on the riskless return to be the lowest and safest rate of return available in the market.

In many cases, however, the rate of return on Treasuries is lower than our hurdle rate. If a pension fund were to invest solely in Treasuries, it would either have to have a longer planning period targeted to attain full funding, or it would have to rely on larger contributions to make up for the shortfall. In practice, many pension liabilities will always mature in the longer term and may be properly invested in riskier assets because there is plenty of time to recover from any losses that might be experienced. Other pension liabilities are much shorter term, and Treasuries might be perfectly appropriate to cover these obligations. Remember that the hurdle rate is a balance sheet integration device and only one (albeit an important one) of a number of tools we can use to allocate assets and judge questions of risk and return.

It is also true that markets change and that one level of return can be earned at one point in time at a certain level of risk, while at another point in time we might have to take much higher risks to obtain the same return. This fact makes it impractical to consider the hurdle rate of return as a ceiling return. Instead, it is the overall big-picture return objective that we have calculated as required to fully fund the pension plan within a set investment horizon. It is a type of compass that gives us direction in navigating through the capital markets. As we consider our choice of assets in this light, there are several important factors that must be kept in view. These factors include our funded ratio, the timing and size of our liabilities, and the asset mix we have relative to our liabilities. The interplay among these factors at any point in time in the capital markets determines the level of success we will have in reaching the objective of becoming fully funded.

## BASIC CHARACTERISTICS OF DEBT AND EQUITY

As mentioned previously, the two principal investable asset classes are debt and equity. How we arrive at optimal levels of debt and equity in the portfolio depends on many variables. Nevertheless, the fundamental characteristics of debt and equity don't change. And, while it is true that equities have historically given superior total returns over time than debt, it is equally true that the certainty of those returns, at any point in time, is far less assured with equity than it is with debt.

The inherently high cash flows available to the debtholder are coupled with automatic liquidation in the form of principal repayment. If the debt is of high quality and one intends to hold the fixed income security to maturity, we know what it is worth today and what it will be worth throughout its life. And, as we will see, it is that certainty that must be relied on when the safety of nearer-term pension benefit payments is our objective. Accordingly, as we strive to get a hit for every at bat, we should consider the following as guiding principles:

1. We can be more certain of funding pension liabilities using current income and principal repayments from high-quality fixed-income securities than from dividends and capital gains on stocks. This is because dividends and capital gains on stocks are less certain at any moment in time than the income and principal repayment from high-quality fixed-income securities.

2. Asset allocations to equities should be inversely proportionate to the need for cash to fund benefits of retiring members. That is, all other factors being equal, the greater the number of beneficiaries who are approaching retirement age, the lower the percentage of stocks we should have in our portfolio.

3. Asset allocations to fixed-income securities should be directly proportionate to the need for cash to fund benefits of retiring members. That is, all other factors being equal, the greater the number of beneficiaries who are approaching retirement age, the higher the percentage of fixed-income securities we should have in our portfolio.

It is important to note that the deliberate use of equities to improve long-term rates of return implies that capital gains in equities must be converted into fixed-income securities to fund pension benefits as liabilities move into the intermediate and short term. This process involves an investment technique known as a sell discipline. In its most simple form, a sell discipline is a group of rules to be followed by an investor in deciding when to sell an asset. In the pension fund world, a sell discipline is a strategy to sell assets in a premeditated fashion to meet the financial objective related to paying all current and future pension obligations when and as they fall due. In most pension funds today, a sell discipline requires rare courage and fortitude to implement.

Again, board members must be aware and sensitive to their impulse to search for ever higher returns on pension investments. We cannot blithely assume that pension fund board members are immune to this very real human emotion. There is an undeniable urge to believe that if we adopt a lower risk profile in pension fund portfolio management, one is, as the saying goes, leaving money on the table. The historically higher rates of return on equities drive this thinking, which goes something like this: If equities give a higher return than fixed-income securities, then a portfolio should be heavily weighted toward equities. The trouble with this approach is that it has nothing to do with paying the pensions. The level of equities in a portfolio, or of any other higher risk, higher return security, must not be driven by greed. Instead, it must be driven by the need to fully fund and pay pension obligations. Equities have a place in virtually every pension fund portfolio. But the proportion of equities to fixed income must always be judged in relation to the need to pay specific pension liabilities. A singular desire to rack up ever-higher paper returns has no place in the world of the pension fund board member, who must realize specific gains to pay out specific obligations.

Regardless of whether a pension fund's financial objectives are re-lated or unrelated to the structure and timing of its liabilities, we must deal with math, or at least higher order arithmetic, to be able to measure any type of performance. Often, these numbers can appear overwhelmingly complex. In most pension funds, numbers, and judgments about numbers, are at the core of the information a board member is likely to receive. Let's explore this topic further.

## $(R_{1i}\text{-}R_1 \text{ ave}) \times (R_{2i}\text{-}R_2 \text{ ave})$

What is it about numbers? Are they friend or foe? How can we find meaning in them? And, in the world of investment managers and consultants, how do we avoid being overwhelmed by number mania? Maybe number mania would be easier to describe if we slip into something less comfortable:

$$[(2.3)^{n-4} + (1-i_x-4.67) + (r_1 + r_2 + \ldots r_n + 1)]$$

The above nonsense formula doesn't further understanding because num-bers in and of themselves don't solve problems or necessarily communicate anything of substance. If we say that a jar of milk has a liquid capacity of 231 cubic inches, what does that mean to us? On the other hand, if we ask ourselves about a gallon of milk, we can then understand how much milk is in question. Numbers are only meaningful when we can relate them to something we already understand.

Yet when we hear about numerically expressed concepts like standard deviation, covariance, beta, and the like, what are we supposed to think? Numbers can become imbued with an undeserved power, holding us in their sway even though we might not fully understand what they mean. Number mania is widespread in the world of pension funds, but what do the numbers tell us about paying pensions? Virtually all pension managers, academics, and consultants produce numbers and formulae representing collections of data not directly connected to the job of paying the pensions. That's strong language, you say. But it's true. Without placing the numbers into a context that relates to paying pensions, how can we make sense of what the numbers mean?

## THE RELEVANCE OF NUMBERS

In the world of pension funds, there are two types of numbers—those directly related to paying pensions and those indirectly related to paying pensions. Let's look at each type.

Directly relevant numbers are a little like a car's headlights on a dark night. They help us see where we are going. An actuary produces extremely useful numbers in the calculation of the size and timing of our projected liabilities. Without the actuary's calculations, we cannot determine other useful numbers such as our hurdle rate of return, our funded ratio, our cost of funding, cash coverage ratios, or other measures of progress in reaching and maintaining a fully funded status ready to pay all the pensions as they fall due. The actuary calculates numbers that can be used to measure *pension management performance*.

Indirectly relevant numbers are not directly connected with the task of paying pensions. These numbers rarely give us important insights into reaching and maintaining a fully funded status. Highest on the list of indirectly relevant numbers are the quarter-to-quarter, year-to-year, manager-to-manager investment performance comparisons with the indexes. Yet these are the numbers trotted out in front of board members and paraded around with great fanfare by consultants and managers alike. These numbers are important, but they are less important that the numbers that tell us how we are doing in the effort to pay pensions at the lowest cost and risk. Typically, these numbers measure *investment management performance*.

The objective of pension fund management is to pay and prepare to pay all pension benefits at the lowest cost to the contributors and the lowest risk of nonpayment of benefits to the plan participants. For pension funds, investment management must involve numerical performance assessments that make comparisons among managers and between each manager and the capital markets. However, pension fund management itself involves measurement of the pace of progress being made by a pension fund in striving to meet its financial objective of paying and preparing to pay pension benefits at the lowest cost and risk.

Performance numbers as now construed are not directly connected to the task of paying pensions. But these numbers are not useless. They are interesting to look at and important in helping pension funds manage investment portfolios. Yet, because these performance numbers don't tell us how we are faring in the struggle to reach and maintain full funding at the lowest cost and risk, they can obscure our mission as pension fund stewards.

## DECISION MAKING BY THE NUMBERS

Numbers are put to another purpose, which can serve to confuse many pension fund board members. These numbers have to do with the application of complicated mathematics to the job of pension fund management. At heart, this effort attempts to organize and manage by mathematic prescription. It is a tempting but flawed strategy. The impulse to apply numeric solutions to every situation is an attempt to deal with uncertainty by making it seem more certain. Remember a number of years ago, the Federal Reserve Board declared that it could fine-tune the economy? This fine tuning was based on the premise that the Fed knew enough about the economy to steer its course under all circumstances. This may yet be possible, but we haven't seen it to date. Another example of this approach was in the world of econometrics, where practitioners confidently predicted their ability to fully describe the world's economies with mathematic models.

You see, investment management is not really a science; not yet, anyway. Investment management involves social behavior, and social behavior has not been adequately investigated to determine whether or not it follows any predictable courses over time. The application of mathematics and statistics to investments conveys the impression that investing is scientific. But investment management is not truly scientific, despite the fascination with numbers and statistics.


## WHAT CAUSES WHAT

The pursuit of science depends on using what is known as the empirical method to determine causality, or what causes what. The empirical method attempts to establish causes for phenomena through repeatable experiments. Variables are isolated, with some being held constant, and others changed to note the effect on the outcome of the experiment. Then, once armed with causal knowledge, we influence the world through actions that have predictable consequences. But, while ever-more-complex formulas can be constructed in the attempt to predict the investment future, none of these pursuits approach the predictability of, say, chemistry or electronics.

This is not to say that at some point in the future aggregate human behavior might not become more predictable. Certainly, the advent of computers will continue to revolutionize our ability to deal with enormous quantities of data in increasingly sophisticated ways. Yet, movements in the capital markets are not entirely predictable today, particularly over relatively short periods of time, and pension fund board members would do well to be skeptical of those who claim otherwise. The quantitative approach to investment management is useful but must be applied with judgment and common sense. Mathematic gymnastics in and of themselves don't address the more difficult issues involved in paying pensions.

There is a tendency among many in finance to think, "If I had just one more fact, I would then be able to predict the next move in the market." Unfortunately, life does not seem to yield its secrets that easily. The investment world seems to have too many interrelated variables to isolate causality. These innumerable variables are so interconnected that exact prediction becomes difficult, if not impossible. Instead, the careful application of common sense, intuition, and judgment are the paramount considerations for board members. To believe otherwise avoids the hard work of investment management.

The tendency for investment professionals to use analytical tweezers in a rigorously mathematic fashion obscures our windshield as we drive in the dark night without headlights. And, when the windshield is covered with numbers, we cannot see well enough to drive to our destination. Board members must be on guard not to fall prey to number mania. Numbers often represent undigested information that is of little use in helping make sense of true stewardship obligations.

## THE CONSULTANT'S PERFORMANCE REPORT

While there are exceptions, many pension fund consultants often focus on investment performance numbers without satisfying the board's hunger for more substantive information about the central mission of the fund. Many board members may not even know that a consultant's report often measures only the performance of asset managers and is not intended to speak to the financial needs and objectives of the fund.

Yet, for a wide variety of reasons, pension fund consultants have become a fixture in most pension funds. The board, looking to discharge its fiduciary responsibility, engages consultants to help interpret the best course to follow through the investment world and measure the returns obtained by various investments. In many pension funds, the consultant's performance report is a regular, periodic occurrence. But, as we will see, investment performance and pension fund performance are two very different issues. Let's peek in on a consultant's presentation that did not go as planned.

The board had just finished lunch and were settling down to hear what the consultant, Mr. Cal Q. Late, had to say about the performance of the pension fund's portfolio. The report was as thick as a phone book and none of the board members had had the time to look through it. It had been sent in advance of the board meeting because together the books were too thick for the consultant to lug around without a wheelbarrow. Mr. Late had brought overhead transparencies and walked to the front of the board room to begin his presentation.

The board had been through this before. A review of the quarterly performance report is a board ritual. A few of them were idly thumbing through the thick reports, looking at this chart and that table, not really focusing on any specific page. Cal began with what one board member referred to as the star charts. These were charts with many dots on them, showing which managers fell where in the "universe" of similar managers with respect to returns and standard deviation of returns. Fixed income came first. The consultant reviewed the managers' quarterly, year-to-date, and five-year performance against each other, against inflation, and, most importantly, against the Shearson Lehman Government Corporate Index. The board members simply looked on. Mr. Late moved on to the equities, where he went through the same drill. Managers were compared to each other and to several indexes. On and on Cal droned, talking about beta, volatility, risk-adjusted returns, styles of management, market trends, and the like.

As the consultant continued, several pension fund board members appeared to have some difficulty paying attention. It wasn't that they were bored; it was just that the volume of information was overwhelming. If we could listen to the board members think, what was going through their heads? What was it they were supposed to be looking for? Couldn't this information be expressed in a simpler form? One pension fund board member thought to himself that some of their managers who were investment gurus were really resting on their laurels. Another thought about whether it was possible to tell how much money a manager had made for the pension fund. Several others were a little embarrassed that they didn't really understand all the data being thrown at them.

Performance is possibly the most perplexing subject facing board members. Yet the consultant wasn't making things any better. He continued on and on, talking about the tools of his craft, using the buzzwords developed by investment folks to describe their labors. Then one board member, feeling particularly bold, dropped a bombshell into the consultant's presentation. He asked, "What do all these performance numbers have to do with paying the pensions?"

Cal stopped. A hush fell over the room. After a pause, Cal explained, as if to a child, that the quarterly investment performance report is an important indication of how well the pension fund's portfolio was performing. The emboldened board member asked, "Well, how well are we doing, then? Why don't you just tell us."

The consultant responded by saying that a number of the fund's managers had outperformed their indexes, and a number of them had not. He started to explain about who had fallen into the top quartile of which universe when the board member stopped him by saying, "You are repeating yourself. We already heard all that stuff. Just tell us what your measurements have to do with paying the pensions. I mean, are we gaining or losing?" Patiently, Cal began to explain that the fund had indeed made money the previous quarter and that its assets increased by some 3.4 percent, a good quarter by any measure.

Not to be deterred, this board member pushed forward dauntlessly. "But have we earned enough to be cutting into our unfunded liability? Have we earned enough to lower the contributions next year? How are we fixed for cash to cut pension checks? I mean, we are in business to fund and pay pensions, right? How are we doing in that regard? Have we planned everything well enough to meet our obligations?"

Cal was stunned. He didn't know what to say. Finally, he muttered that the task of figuring out contributions really belonged to the actuaries, and he wasn't very familiar with the pension fund's actuarial situation.

The performance problem was exposed. In frustration, the brave board member had hit upon the key to performance measurement. It wasn't to be found in the manager comparisons to an index or to each other. Neither was it to be found in the plan's relationship to other plans. It wasn't even to be found in the comparison to an inflation index. Interesting as all these measurements are, they don't begin to describe real pension fund performance.

Real performance for a pension fund measures the fund's ability to pay pensions. We determine this ability to pay pensions by examining the relationships among a pension fund's assets, contributions, and liabilities. Pension fund performance measurement will show how well a plan reduces its cost of funding, increases its funded ratio, and provides the liquidity necessary to actually make the benefit payments when due. Any method of performance measurement that neglects these issues cannot tell us how the pension fund is progressing in its effort to meet its financial obligations.

But if the consultants are often missing the boat and are unprepared to deal with the relationship between a pension fund's liabilities and its assets, what about money managers? How do the asset managers fit into the scheme of things, and what is their proper role in achieving the financial objectives of the fund? Let's consider the manager environment and how managers fit into the puzzle.

## CHASING THE RABBIT

Have you ever seen a greyhound race? The dogs are placed in the gates and spectators wager cash on the outcome. When the gates are opened, the greyhounds leap forward with all the speed they can muster and set off in hot pursuit of their quarry. But what is the object of their chase? How do the spectators measure the success of the race? The curious analogy of a greyhound race drives a wooden stake deep into the heart of modern investment practice. Let's see how.

Greyhounds are fast on their feet. Deep within their dog brains are instinctive responses to the hunt. People harnessed the greyhounds' instincts for the hunt and trained the dogs to run races for sport and profit. How these races are run is enormously instructive. The greyhounds no longer run after prey. Instead, they chase a mechanical rabbit. This contrivance is scented to excite the dogs, and they streak around the track in hot pursuit of their unattainable target. The greyhounds never catch the rabbit because catching the rabbit is not what the race is about. No, greyhound races are about money. The gamblers want to see their dog cross the finish line first, second, or at least show and win money as a result.

Those who manage money on behalf of pension funds are also in a race of sorts. And, while these people are not chasing a mechanical rabbit, they are chasing equally elusive targets. They, too, are extensively trained. Deep within the human brain seems to be a need to compete and win. Money managers compete with each other for clients' money, and winning those competitions means chasing an index "rabbit" better than other money managers. But, as in the greyhound race, the money managers' quarry is not connected to their clients' needs because chasing an index has nothing to do with the financial objectives of a pension fund.

An emphasis on managing assets to pay pensions is very different from the way money management is practiced today. But mere rarity does not diminish the need to manage pension assets responsibly. Responsible pension fund asset management is not beating an index or a peer group. Instead, it is the management of assets in service of the specific financial objective of paying and preparing to pay all the pension benefits without fail as they fall due at the lowest true cost to the contributors and lowest risk of nonpayment of benefits to the plan participant. This objective requires that the pension fund have enough cash to meet current benefit payments, and manage asset growth to prepare to pay projected benefit payments.

Chasing an index is similar to the greyhounds' pursuit of a mechanical rabbit. Today's money managers are running a race with an illusory finish line that differs radically from the true finish line. Like the greyhounds, they are unaware of their circumstances, not even knowing what they don't know. At a greyhound track, it is the responsibility of those who manage the track and the dogs to ensure that the greyhounds cross the finish line. They don't let the dogs decide when and how to run. Neither do they allow the dogs the freedom to decide what to chase.

At the risk of offending those who manage assets for pension funds, board members must not let their dogs run free either. Board members must put the "greyhounds" in service of the greater financial objective of paying the pensions. We must establish rules and norms by which we expect our managers to work, and then see to it that the best interests of the pension fund are served in the process. However, unlike the situation at the dog track, in the investment world, answers are not simple. Investment managers are not greyhounds. For the most part, they are well educated, bright, well motivated, highly paid human beings. But they should be managing money on behalf of their clients' real needs and not merely chasing an index or only trying to beat their peer group.

The present situation is not the fault of money managers. They are hired to serve a purpose and do so under the direction of the board. Because their purpose has been limited, managers and consultants have not been able or willing to offer a more integrated vision of their function. And perhaps this is as it should be. Since managers are but hired hands, the board must be the progenitor of any integrated vision.

Unfortunately, by choice and circumstance, neither consultants nor money managers themselves are in the position to advise board members on these matters. To some degree, this reluctance has a commercial foundation. These people have been collecting millions of dollars in fees to chase the wrong rabbit. It seems highly unlikely that they will change their ways any time soon, because by doing so they will have to admit that they have been very wrong in their approach. This admission would reveal the stark fact that money managers and consultants do not understand what their clients need. No group would commit this sort of commercial suicide.

Actuaries are similarly in no position to advise pension fund board members on integrated asset management. Their perspective, while more realistic than that of the consultants and money managers, nevertheless deals only with one side of the balance sheet. Actuaries know little about the capital markets. However, while the actuaries are in no position to provide integrated services, they are closer in temperament than the investment professionals to begin the slow move back to reality.

What is needed is a new type of financial professional with an interdisciplinary approach. This new type of professional must understand the meaning of true money management and be able to integrate the needs of an institution and coordinate the effort to fulfill those needs within the realm of the capital markets. Only the pension fund board members are in the position to ask for this kind of integrated approach. Managers, consultants, and actuaries will follow the leads of those who pay them and respond only to those challenges demanded of them.

# CHAPTER 3

---

# AN EYE ON THE BASICS

---

The fundamentals of investing have not changed much over the years, even though layers of complexity have been added to the financial world during the 20th century. Yet more complex answers are not necessarily better answers. Elegant solutions will more often be simple than complicated, despite the best efforts of the experts to get bogged down in confusing and contradictory complexities. Because as board members we are called upon to use our common sense to understand the financial world, it is helpful to step back and review certain fundamental concepts of investing. Foremost among those concepts is the power of time and compounding.

## COMPOUNDING OVER TIME—THE KEYSTONE
## OF INVESTING

The speed of change has made our world appear more complicated. In meeting the challenge of complexity we have sought out technological fix-its to help us control our lives and the events affecting them. Unfortunately, sometimes the treatment compounds the problem. Technological complexity often begets confusion. The fruits of confusion are decisions made without a sense of direction or vision. The result is a system of chaos of our own making. The world of investing has its own Rube Goldberg contrivances. Here are a few that have been concocted in the blessed name of investment performance:

- Portfolio insurance.
- Tactical asset allocation.
- Sector rotation.

- Theme management.
- Amplified alpha.

This is just a sampling. The list of sophisticated techniques contrived to handle the complexity of our financial chores is lengthy. Yet, despite all the mental gymnastics, something is missing. That missing element is a sense of understanding how the investment process works. In our fast-paced world, things seem to be getting more complex and more difficult to understand. Is this an illusion or reality? It is hard to tell. The world of finance *seems* more complex than it has ever been. In the eagerness to embrace what seems advanced, pension fund board members must take pains to use and act on commonsense experience. While common sense is anything but common, it often works wonders in cutting through complexities that seem on the verge of overwhelming us from time to time. To get to the heart of the matter, let's rethink and restate the investment problem in simple terms.

## THE POWER OF COMPOUNDING

To illustrate the simple approach, let's borrow from Richard Russell in his "Dow Theory Letters" of May 4, 1988. In that publication, Mr. Russell reminded us of an observation on investing based on time and compounding. Since it is the keystone of investing and stewardship, it is worth repeating here:

> A brilliant investor friend of mine told us many years ago, "Forget timing; just give me time." This fellow was a compounder, a man who knew that assets compound and increase through time.
>
> I learned that lesson on my own, and I learned it early. I learned it from the final article written by the financial editor of the old *New York Herald Tribune*. The editor wrote that, financially, young people make a great mistake. They get married, buy a house and furniture, and thereupon immediately go heavily into *debt*. Then they spend the rest of their lives paying off the debt while going into additional debt.
>
> The intelligent thing to do, stated this editor, is to start saving when you are young. Thus, you will have time and compounding working for—rather than against you. I won't go into all my compounding statistics at this point, but I will offer one example: Put $5,000 a year into high-grade, tax-free muni bonds yielding 7%, and in 20 years you'll have $205,000.

There are two items to remember in the above equation. The first is you must buy high-grade bonds, bonds that are not going to default. That's important. You're not going to make money if you accumulate and compound bankruptcies.

The second thing to remember is . . . you've got to continue buying. You must stay with your program. You can't stop because the market declined or because your next-door neighbor told you that bonds are going out of style.

It should be understood that any other form of investing (and very few people realize this) is an attempt to *beat time*. In other words, any method such as buying stocks or bonds in bear markets and selling out in bull markets, or trading on the basis of buying undervalued stocks and selling when they become overvalued, or any other method, is in reality an effort to beat the compounding process. In attempting to speed up the mathematic certainty of compounding, you are saying, "I'm not going to go the boring compounding-through-time route—I'm going to beat time with shrewd buying and selling."

Now I'm not saying this can't be done. Thousands of investors have done it—and are doing it. But I am saying that in my opinion, most people would be far more successful compounding their way to riches than they would be trying to beat time in the market.[1]

The important point Mr. Russell makes is that the concept of time and compounding is the keystone of any responsible investment policy. Other investment alternatives must establish themselves as improvements upon this simple, uncomplicated approach to reaching desired investment objectives. In our effort to manage other people's money, we have to remind ourselves that sometimes the simplest and most straightforward approach is best. Answers do not have to be modern and sophisticated to be correct.

Before we move on to another view of Mr. Russell's observation, it should be pointed out that Mr. Russell also touches on other cardinal rules of stewardship. These are:

1. The need for savings.
2. The need for discipline.
3. The need for quality in investments.
4. The need to understand the concept of time and its application to investment practice.

---

[1]Reprinted by permission of Richard Russell.

5. The need to understand the power, scope, and depth of compounding.
6. How a controlled and deliberate process of buying *and* selling assets is viewed.

While we won't spend much time elaborating these points here, they serve as excellent additional topics of discussion in the search for a broader understanding of stewardship.

## A MEASURED-STEPS INVESTMENT POLICY

It is all too easy to forget the power of patient compounding when we are focused on the notion of making brilliant leaps of investment prowess. We like to feel as though we and our selected agents are brighter and more perceptive than the rest of the world. As investors, we sometimes believe that we deserve to do better than the rest of the world in our investment activities. We can convince ourselves that we can select assets and managers whose results are spectacular. This belief can drive in a constant search for brilliantly conceived and executed investment strategies. Yet making brilliant leaps of investment decision making is antithetical to the notion of carefully planned prudent action. And carefully planned prudent action is at the very core of pension fund management. Instead of brilliant leaps, then, it is far more advisable for a pension fund board to pursue a methodical "measured-steps" approach to investing.

A measured-steps investment policy touches directly on this concept of beating time. Because stewardship is directed to specific financial objectives, it is equally attentive to this concept of time and compounding. Stewardship sees risk as a function of a consequence—the loss of principal. And, when attempting to compare and evaluate investment alternatives, a straightforward process of compounding must serve as a benchmark for any analysis of the risks or rewards of various options. Put another way, as stated by the well-known dictum of Charles Ellis of Greenwich Associates, the difference between successful investors and unsuccessful investors is a matter of who makes the *fewest mistakes* over the long run.[2]

---

[2]Charles Ellis, *Investment Policy: Winning the Loser's Game* (Homewood, Ill.: Dow Jones-Irwin, 1986).

Making fewer mistakes has a number of important implications for the development of the most successful investment attitude. Often, mistakes can best be avoided through careful planning, calm attention to the task of monitoring, and patience not to act precipitously.

In point of fact, many times, not acting at all is the best course. It seems clear that selective inaction can actually improve investment performance. In the investment world, it is axiomatic that transactions always have an associated cost. Every time the bag of gold dust changes hands, a little dust falls out for the trader who facilitates the transaction. All other things being equal (which they may never be), the portfolio that trades less will perform better by definition. Thus, buying and selling assets less frequently is a more economical way to manage a portfolio. Lower portfolio turnover tends to improve performance.

Selective inaction can also prevent an investor from making as many mistakes. The reason is simple. If the probability of success is 50-50 on a single event, and 50-50 on a second event, the chance that *both* events will occur successfully is only 25 percent. If you continue out to five events, the odds of all *five* occurring successfully will drop to a little more than 3 percent. And, just by continuing to act, we do not always increase the probabilities of success as much as we might suppose. Take something whose chance of success is 1 in 100, for example. If the odds remain the same each time we try to succeed, at what point can we *absolutely be sure* that we will succeed? The real answer is that we can never be absolutely sure, but the probabilities are interesting to contemplate. If you try to succeed over the course of 10 trials, you only have a 10.5 percent chance of success. With 25 trials, you have a 22 percent chance of success. After 50 trials, you have almost a 50-50 chance of success. But, to be 99.9 percent sure of success, you have to have 688 trials. Naturally, the world is more complicated than these simple examples of probability, but the fundamental principle remains. Too much activity can increase the chance of making mistakes, and does not always increase the chances for success.

## DIFFERENCES IN RETURNS BETWEEN STOCKS AND FIXED-INCOME SECURITIES

In an academic sense, Mr. Russell's concept of beating time prompts an important question. Given the power of compounding and the incremental differences in the pattern of returns of stocks versus fixed-income securi-

**TABLE 3–1**
**Incremental Returns**

|  | Stocks versus Fixed-Income Securities | | | |
|---|---|---|---|---|
|  | 12/25 to 6/87 | 12/47 to 6/87 | 12/65 to 6/87 | 12/72 to 6/87 |
| 100% stocks | 9.89% | 11.24% | 10.12% | 11.67% |
| 100% bonds | 4.97% | 4.72% | 6.98% | 8.73% |
| Difference | 4.92% | 6.52% | 3.14% | 2.94% |

Source: Evaluation Associates, Inc.

**TABLE 3–2**
**Historic Returns**

|  | Average Annual Rate of Return | | | |
|---|---|---|---|---|
|  | 12/25 to 6/87 | 12/47 to 6/87 | 12/65 to 6/87 | 12/72 to 6/87 |
| Common stocks | 9.89% | 11.24% | 10.12% | 11.67% |
| Long corp. bonds | 4.97% | 4.72% | 6.98% | 8.73% |
| T-bills | 3.41% | 4.56% | 7.16% | 8.16% |
| C.P.I. | 2.97% | 4.40% | 6.01% | 6.90% |
| Time period | 61.5 yrs. | 41.5 yrs. | 21.5 yrs. | 14.5 yrs. |

Source: Evaluation Associates, Inc.

ties, what proportional mix of debt and equity makes the most sense for a pension fund investor? Table 3–1 is a statistical view we can use to better define the issue.

Studying the incremental returns of stocks in Table 3–1 above, one might conclude that the risk premium is so wide that a heavy concentration in equities is always warranted. And, if we look at the historic returns in Table 3–2, we can see that the same argument for equities seems to be obvious.

Tables 3–1 and 3–2 only examine the issue from the two extremes, either 100 percent equities or 100 percent fixed-income securities. As we

**TABLE 3–3**
**Historic Returns**

| | | Stocks and Fixed-Income Securities | | | |
|---|---|---|---|---|---|
| Stocks | Bonds | 12/25 to 6/87 | 12/47 to 6/87 | 12/65 to 6/87 | 12/72 to 6/87 |
| 100% | 0% | 9.89% | 11.24% | 10.12% | 11.67% |
| 75% | 25% | 9.07% | 9.86% | 9.54% | 11.18% |
| 50% | 50% | 7.97% | 8.32% | 8.83% | 10.53% |
| 25% | 75% | 6.60% | 6.61% | 7.97% | 9.71% |
| 0% | 100% | 4.97% | 4.72% | 6.98% | 8.73% |
| Time period | | 61.5 yrs. | 41.5 yrs. | 21.5 yrs | 14.5 yrs. |

Source: Evaluation Associates, Inc.

change the mix of these asset classes, the spreads narrow, as shown in Table 3–3.

Given the above data, why does anyone invest in fixed income at all? The answer is severalfold. First, and most importantly, the returns from high-quality bonds are *assured*. That is, if we buy a high-quality bond and hold it to maturity, we will be paid interest and principal as promised. Stocks, on the other hand, give no assurance about anything. If, when you need the money from an equity investment, the stock's price is down, tough luck. Holding bonds gives many a pension fund board member a great deal of well-earned peace of mind. Second, while we will discuss an alternative approach, in the current scheme of things, many investors rely on the fact that a portfolio of bonds will outperform a portfolio of stocks during certain periods. Prediction of those periods is difficult, but the fact is that these periods do occur. Finally, the prices of stocks and bonds do not always move in the same direction at the same time. That is, at any point in time, when returns from a portfolio of bonds improve, sometimes returns from a stock portfolio improve and sometimes they don't. And, as we will see, this notion of correlation among investment returns forms the basis for much of modern institutional investment practice.

But, regardless of these considerations, in today's pension funds, board members mix stocks and bonds in portfolios with the sole objective of return maximization. Squeezing maximum returns from an investment portfolio might be a worthwhile pursuit if we are *absolutely certain* that we can pay our obligations as they fall due. As we will see, these objectives are not mutually exclusive, but to manage them properly requires foresight and planning on the part of pension fund board members.

But before we turn to the problem of how to construct a pension portfolio in a responsible fashion, we need to examine the basic characteristics of fixed-income and equity securities.

## FIXED-INCOME SECURITIES AND SOOTHSAYERS

Now that we have looked at some of the basic historic data and considered a few of the facts about stocks and bonds, let's look at each category of security in terms of its basic characteristics. Fixed-income securities are often thought of as being dull and reliable when compared to their flashier competition over in the stock markets. And, before the junk bond craze hit corporate America, bonds were pretty dull and reliable. Most bonds still are.

We all know that a bond is nothing more than the promise of a borrower to pay the lender's principal back, and to pay the lender interest for use of the money during the life of the loan. That much is easy to understand and agree upon. What's also easy to understand is what we saw in the previous section, that, historically, fixed-income securities have tended to have lower returns than stocks. What's not as well understood is the fact that active bond management, which involves buying and selling fixed-income securities in search of capital gains, is not a good game for the pension fund to play with great vigor on a regular basis. Let's see why.

## A FEW FUNDAMENTALS ABOUT BONDS

Bond obligations are only as good as the creditworthiness of the issuer. When a bond issuer makes a promise to pay interest, and fails to do so, obviously the bondholder will earn less than he anticipated when the bonds were purchased. When a bond issuer makes a promise to pay principal, and fails to do so, obviously the bondholder will suffer a loss of that principal. Yet if the issuer of the bonds makes good on the promise to pay both interest and principal, the bond buyer who buys a newly issued bond and holds it to maturity will receive exactly what he has been promised, nothing more and nothing less.

When interest rates go up, the market prices of bonds will fall. This is a simple fact of the marketplace. Here's why. If, as a bond buyer, we can get a better return on bonds that are newly issued at higher interest rates than the lower rates on bonds issued yesterday, we will be motivated to buy the new bonds rather than the old ones. Therefore, the prices of the old bonds must be lowered so that any purchaser of those old bonds will, over the remaining life of the bonds, receive the same amount of income from the interest payments and the full principal payments as prevailed in the market when the old bonds were purchased. A reverse process occurs when interest rates fall and the prices of previously issued bonds increase.

There are many interesting and worthwhile observations about bonds related to the rise and fall of interest rates. Bond interest rates are made up of several components. There is the real interest rate, the expected (or implicit) inflation rate, and there is a risk premium. The real interest rate involves the rental rate on the borrowed money. This is the bond investor's nominal return. Added to this is the expected inflation rate. The purchasing power of the bond investor's capital will diminish unless the bond investor is compensated for the expectation of inflation. Finally, there is a risk premium. The risk premium is divided into two parts. There is credit risk, which involves the risk of nonpayment of interest or principal. And there is reinvestment rate risk, which involves the rate at which a bond buyer can reinvest his interest income as that income is received.

As long as we are looking at various bond fundamentals, we should also consider the concept of bond duration. Duration is nothing more than the average amount of time, measured in years, it takes for an investor to recover his initial investment. Duration has an interesting feature. The duration of a bond can tell us how much movement there will be in a bond's price for a given movement in interest rates. In fact, the duration of a bond actually tells the bond investor the percentage a bond's price will increase or decrease for each 1 percent change in interest rates. A bond with a duration of eight years will move up 8 percent in price when interest rates fall 1 percent. It's almost mystical, isn't it? Consideration of the relationship between duration and price changes shows us that bonds with longer maturities are more sensitive to changes in interest rates than bonds with shorter maturities. Additionally, the higher the coupon and the longer the maturity of the bond, the more reinvestment rate risk there is.

As we can see, the entire mechanism driving movements in the prices of fixed-income securities depends on movements in interest rates. The corollary to this fact is that most active bond managers must attempt to predict interest rate movements in their effort to consistently generate capital gains in a fixed-income portfolio. How hard is it to predict interest rate movements? Well, it depends on whom we ask. If we ask a bond manager, he will probably tell us that his ultra-sophisticated 68 variable computer model will be able to predict interest rate movements 83.54 percent of the time. But can he? The evidence seems to indicate that he cannot. Interest rate predictions are a bit like weather forecasts. Nobody impugns the efforts of the weather forecasters, but we all take their predictions with a grain of salt. And, like weather forecasting, it is possible (though by no means yet proven) that interest rate forecasting might get better over time.

The best explanation for the difficulties faced in predicting interest rate movements is embedded in the very structure of the bond market itself. These markets, particularly the government bond markets, are exceedingly efficient. That is, there are very few opportunities to exploit discrepancies between the market value and the intrinsic value of a government bond, because, in practice, such discrepancies tend to be small. This is probably because hordes of bond traders, analysts, and portfolio managers are all focused on a single variable: interest rates. This extraordinary obsession with one variable results in few circumstances where one participant can outsmart another. Thus, over time, outperforming the overall bond markets becomes a more or less futile task.

Yet, notwithstanding the difficulties of predicting interest rates, bond managers still keep trying. These managers will often trade their bonds regularly as they place their bets on the upward or downward movements in rates. The folly of this regular trading activity is perhaps best shown by the fact that from the inception of the Shearson Lehman Government Bond Index, to the end of 1989 there was a negative 2.27 percent return from price changes, and a 330.26 percent return from coupon and reinvestment. The message is clear: don't churn the fixed-income portfolio in search of capital gains. In point of fact, because of the structure of the bond market, trading bonds has another danger we will examine later in more detail—hidden transaction costs.

So, instead of trading bonds, how should they be used in a pension portfolio? The answer is simple but boring. In the main, bond portfolios should be constructed to provide a means to fund our liabilities. These securities should be held patiently rather than traded frenetically. If the creditworthiness of the issuer is high, most bonds should be designed around a buy-and-hold strategy.

Common stocks are another matter. Investigations into these strange securities usually generate more heat than light.

## LET'S CONFRONT COMMON STOCKS HEAD-ON

Have you ever noticed how people behave when they have just had one too many? They aren't falling down drunk, but they are often noticeably more straightforward and honest about their observations concerning a wide variety of things. While this is not always a good practice, neither is it invariably a bad one. Sometimes we can learn a lot when our inhibitions are allowed to relax, and our guard is down a bit. Let's get into our cups a bit, then, about, of all things, common stocks.

If this sounds like a strange idea, then let's explore it a little. The intent is to confront commonly held opinions with an honest and straightforward approach. But before we get off the subject of drinking, there is another point to make here that will later relate directly back to common stocks. When I was in college, my economics professor used to talk about the marginal propensity of consumption. While I don't pretend to have been a great scholar, I think I learned this lesson pretty well. Essentially, the concept states that the first beer always tastes better than the second, and the second better than the third, and fourth, and so on.

Often, we can learn many interesting things about life's more confusing issues by asking the simplest and most fundamental of questions. But we must be blunt and we must not be embarrassed to challenge orthodoxy. (I don't know about you, but when I was drinking those beers in college, I expressed myself in a very blunt fashion.) With common stocks, the most fundamental and blunt question we can ask ourselves is this: What are common stocks and why would someone want to invest in them?

Of course, as we all know, each share of common stock is a small piece of ownership of a company. But why would an investor wish to have this ownership? The obvious answer is that an investor wants to own a common stock in order to sell it to someone else at a higher price. But again, we are left with the fundamental question of why the *next* buyer would want to own a small piece of a company at a higher price than was originally paid by the seller. Doesn't this sound like a dog chasing his tail, or a variation of the old search for a greater fool? The truth is that in the short run many stocks go up because of the emotions and market sentiments of greater fools. It seems self-evident, but sometimes stock prices go up simply because there are a lot of investors investing in them.

But this begs the real question of why somebody would want to invest in a common stock in the first place. The real answer is that ownership of a common stock gives the investor the right to share in the earnings stream of the company through dividends. The next investor who purchases the stock wishes to participate in the expansion of those earnings and dividends as the company grows in size and profitability. But with dividends accounting for something around a 3 percent to 4 percent yield, why would anyone invest in common stocks when an investor can easily double those rates of return in many fixed-income investments, without much risk to income or principal? The answer is that the common stock investor is hoping that the perception of future growth in distributable earnings of the issuing company will be compelling enough to persuade others to purchase the shares at ever-increasing prices, creating the potential for capital gains.

Let's see what another observer, John Burr Williams, has to say about common stocks:

> Let us define the investment value of a stock as the present value of all the dividends to be paid upon it . . . To appraise the investment value, then, it is necessary to estimate the future payments. The annuity of payments, adjusted for changes in the value of money itself, may then be discounted at the pure interest rate demanded by the investor.
>
> Most people will object at once to the foregoing formula for stocks by saying that it should use the present worth of future *earnings,* not future *dividends.* But should not earnings and dividends both give the same answer under the implicit assumptions of our critics? If earnings not paid out in dividends are all successfully reinvested at compound interest for the benefit of stockholders, as the critics imply, then these earnings should produce dividends later; if not, they are money lost.
>
> . . . Earnings are only a means to an end, and the means should not be mistaken for the end. Therefore, we must say that a stock derives its value from its dividends, not its earnings. In short, a stock is worth *only what you can get out of it.* Even so spoke the farmer to his son:
>
> > A cow for her milk,
> > A hen for her eggs,
> > And a stock, by heck,
> > For her dividends.

> An orchard for fruit,
> Bees for their honey,
> And stocks, besides,
> For their dividends.

The old man knew where milk and honey came from, but he made no such mistake as to tell his son to buy a cow for her cud or bees for their buzz. (Italics in original.)[3]

Now, there may be those who say that stocks are also bought for some intrinsic worth derived from the excess of the value of the assets of the company as compared to its liabilities. This figure is known as a company's net worth. And, after all, a company's net worth should be worth something to its owners, the shareholders. But how does this net worth figure actually benefit the shareholder if it is not distributed out to the shareholders? There are others who would say that the price of a company's stock must also reflect the net liquidation value of the company's assets, whether or not that liquidation value is adequately represented on the company's books. But unless a company is actually broken up, its assets sold, and the proceeds distributed, liquidation value has no real economic meaning to the shareholders.

While the above description is not a popular one, it appears to be the only explanation that makes sense. But one thing any investor knows is that the capital markets don't always seem to make sense. So what is it about stocks that makes them valued by investors at prices higher than the present value of an estimated future dividend flow? Let's examine this question at greater length.

## MARKET VALUE, UTILITY VALUE, AND PERCEIVED VALUE

While it seems evident that the commonsense approach outlined above appears correct, the fact is that stock market investors are driven by something other than the usefulness, or utility, of owning a common stock for its dividends. As strange as it may seem to a disinterested observer,

---

[3]From John Burr Williams, *The Theory of Investment Value* (Cambridge, Mass.: 1938), as quoted in *Classics: An Investor's Anthology*, ed. Charles D. Ellis with James R. Vertin (Homewood, Ill.: Dow Jones-Irwin, 1989), pp. 153–54.

stock market investors place a premium on the price of a stock corresponding to a variety of circumstances that are apparently unrelated to the generation of dividends.

We might reasonably refer to the price of a stock based on the present value of its projected dividend stream as the *utility value*, because as long as the stock is held, only the dividend payout has utility to the stockholder. The stockholder must sell a stock to someone else to realize any more value from a stock investment other than the dividend. In practice, investors regularly pay more for a stock than its utility value. In effect, a premium is paid over the utility value merely to own the stock. When this premium is added to the utility value, we arrive at the market value for the stock, which represents the total *perceived value* of the shares, in the eyes of the buyer and seller, at the moment they complete the transaction.

But perceived values are often based on emotional judgments, consisting of the aggregate opinions of the group of individuals who trade in the securities in question. Unfortunately, we have not yet been able to predict the direction or strength of these opinions. But if perceived value cannot be predicted, and if dividends and dividend growth tend to underperform bond income and reinvestment, what *can* we be sure of when investing in the stock market? The answer is that, in the long run, we can be sure that the relative performance of one stock to another stock must be driven by fundamental considerations of each company that issues shares for sale to the public.

What do we mean by the term *fundamental considerations?* These considerations relate to a company's ability to generate present or future distributable cash to its shareholders. This ability is, in turn, related to the company's ability to deliver its goods or services to a sufficient number of customers at sufficiently high enough prices to cover the company's costs and expenses and still have some left over. This leftover is profit. Profit can either be reinvested in the business, or it can be distributed to the shareholders. The present and future earnings capacity of the business is related to a wide set of factors which, when taken together, represent the company's fundamental considerations.

These fundamental considerations must be viewed with the understanding that even subjectively perceived values have their limits. These limits are determined by those fundamental factors related to the present and future earnings capacity of a given business. So it should be remembered that while investor perceptions may inflate common stock prices beyond the level of the present value of any foreseeable dividend payouts, that potential inflation of price is not infinite. It would seem reasonable, in fact, to come to the conclusion that common stock prices *have* to be driven by fundamental considerations in the longer run, even though emotion, fads, and market psychology all play a role in the shorter run. Put in another way, over the longer term, as the well-known investment theorist Ben Graham said, "value will out." This value consists of the facts surrounding the company that will enable it to grow its earnings (and, one supposes, distribute more dividends). When a company can grow its earnings, and thus have the capacity to pay out dividends, its share price will be bid up. Conversely, if a company's fortunes are declining, earnings and dividends will be less likely to increase, and may go down or be eliminated altogether. Naturally, share price of company in decline will almost certainly be depressed.

These ideas about common stock are often lumped together in what has come to be known as *value investing*. Value investors typically search out companies with share prices that are perceived to be undervalued relative to the company's fundamentals. Value stocks often have higher-than-average dividend yields because they are earning and paying out more dividends relative to their share price than other stocks. Those familiar with Wall Street might also be familiar with a type of stock investing known as *growth investing*. Growth investors seek to purchase shares in companies with the potential to grow rapidly. Growth investors do not pay much attention to dividend yields. Their companies are reinvesting earnings to further fuel the growth of the company. Yet, to have a utility value, even growth companies must pay out a dividend at some point in the future. Otherwise, even in the long run, there would be no point to holding growth stocks.

Finally, we should remember that perceptions of fundamental forces in the business environment will also tend to move both groups of stocks, as well as the stock market in general. Movements of interest rates, money supply, Gross Domestic Product (GDP) growth, inflation rates, unemployment, and many, many other reported measurements will be assessed by stock market investors as having an effect on the overall climate for corporate prosperity. Similarly, to the degree that political issues are perceived to be positive or negative for business, they will tend to influence the overall climate for stock market investing.

Obviously, the above discussion is not intended to be an overview of stock market investing. Instead, the intention is to try and understand why common stock values are subject to such wide variation in price. As pension fund investors, we have to try to understand these matters to better deal with the opportunities, and the risks, of stock investing. It seems reasonably clear, then, that within certain bounds, common stock prices are driven by the *perception* of fundamental value, rather than by their ability to generate predictable, periodic cash flow in the form of distributed dividends paid to the shareholders. To the degree that this perception of value is related to subjective judgments, stock prices will tend to be more volatile. In today's market, this can be exemplified in the share prices accorded to the biotechnology companies, most of which are long on promise and short on earnings and dividends. Conversely, if a company's fundamental condition is less speculative, if it pays out predictable dividends, its price will tend to be inherently more stable. Good examples of these kinds of stocks include shares issued by utilities, most of which trade within a relatively narrow range and pay out dividends with great regularity.

The bottom line to this discussion is that all stock prices move up and down. What's more, not only do individual stock prices fluctuate, but the overall level of stock market valuations move up and down as well. While in the short run these upward and downward swings are not entirely predictable, in the long run these movements must be driven by fundamental characteristics. But the long run does not pay today's pension benefit. It is the short run that we must rely on to fund short-run obligations. And, because stock values are unpredictable in the short run, it is imprudent for a pension fund investor to be caught holding too many common stocks when near-term benefit payments have to be made.

## DEMOGRAPHIC TRENDS, PENSION FUNDS, AND COMMON STOCKS

Nevertheless, there are countervailing forces in the pension fund world that have propelled the market for certain common stocks forward over the last few years. These trends will create an eventual fork in the road for investors. The demographics driving the contribution to benefit ratios have been lopsided in favor of contributions, giving many pension funds huge amounts of cash to invest. The meaning of this build-up in assets is often neglected, even though it should be self-evident. The pension funds have been getting ready for retirements related to the baby-boom for many years. In this light, it becomes clear that pension funds have been building up huge assets in order to pay out huge pension liabilities. As a result, a large portion of these assets will have to be converted to cash to pay pensions during the coming years.

A study performed in May 1991 by Mr. Barrie Wigmore of Goldman Sachs attempted to quantify the reasons behind the upward movements for the stocks that make up the Standard & Poor's (S&P) 500 for the 10-year period from 1979 to 1989. Mr. Wigmore was able to isolate the effect of interest rates as causing 11 percent of the growth in the S&P 500, earnings estimates as causing 39 percent of the growth, and merger and acquisition activity as causing 12 percent of the growth. The residual 38 percent of the 10-year growth in the S&P 500 was deemed unexplained. Yet it seems entirely likely that Mr. Wigmore simply did not consider pension fund demographics and cash flows in his analysis. While further research is warranted into this area, common sense tells us that when there are more buyers than sellers, prices will tend to go up.

The sheer size of many pension funds drives them to seek out investments with sufficient liquidity to absorb their buying and selling without impacting the market tremendously. That is, no pension fund wants to force the price of a security down when it sells, or force it up when it buys. Additionally, many pension funds have restrictions on the levels of ownership they are permitted to have in any one corporation. As a result of these trends, pension funds have sought out the largest companies to invest in, driving the prices of those stocks up, much of the time beyond the fundamental strength of the underlying growth in distributable earnings. The market value, known as the market capitalization, of all the outstanding shares of each of these big companies is obviously huge, and these stocks are sometimes referred to as *large cap stocks*.

These recent investing trends demonstrate the inverse of my economic professor's theory of the marginal propensity of consumption. The largest companies, which make up the most popular index, the S&P 500, have finite numbers of shares of common stock in the market. So, the big pension funds feel better and better with each additional share of stock that they purchase, regardless of the underlying fundamental value of that stock. This strange occurrence is derived from pension funds themselves pushing up prices of large cap stocks by buying them with fervor. The problem is magnified not only by the investors who passively manage stocks by mirroring an index, but also by the ownership of those same stocks when selected by a manager who has decided to purchase them for other reasons. During 1990 and 1991, many pension fund investors have been attracted to companies with smaller capitalizations, known as *small cap stocks*. As shares of these companies began to get bought up at an increasing rate, prices rose. And once again, the more the pension funds invested in these small cap stocks, the higher the prices went.

It is interesting that as demographics move larger numbers of pension benefit payables closer to the present, many pension funds have been increasing their allocations to common stocks. We previously examined the need for cash to pay pensions, and noted that cash is more predictably generated from fixed income than it is from common stocks. At some point, it seems evident that pension funds will have to switch from equities to fixed income as demographic imperatives force them to have an increasing need for cash to pay pensions. Of course, this need for cash is different for each pension fund investor, depending on their specific circumstances. Pension funds with larger nearer term liabilities will find themselves needing more cash sooner than those with large liabilities looming farther out in the future.

Notwithstanding the demographic implications of the baby-boom generation, the trend among pension funds has been to increase their allocations to common stocks without reference to the liability side of their balance sheets. As has been previously noted, the long-term total rates of return from common stocks (dividends plus capital gains) has been demonstrably higher than the returns from fixed-income securities. Accordingly, many pension funds have decided to place increasingly larger proportions of their portfolios into common stocks so as to generate greater rates of return. However, this asset allocation decision has been made in a vacuum. That is, the decision has been made without regard to the ultimate need for pension funds to generate cash to pay pensions. For pension funds with a high proportion of long-term liabilities, a relatively high equity allocation may be warranted. For pension funds with nearer term liabilities, however, increases in common stock allocations are ill-advised. Figure 3–1 illustrates the two trends in graphic form.

## PENSION FUND INVESTMENT HORIZONS
## AND COMMON STOCKS

Many pension fund investors have assumed that they are only long-term investors. But, as we will discuss in more detail in Chapter 4, pension funds have multiple investment horizons. That is, they have to pay pensions

**FIGURE 3–1**
**Pension Liabilities versus Equity Allocations**

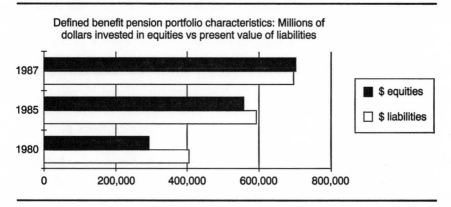

Defined benefit pension portfolio characteristics: Millions of
dollars invested in equities vs present value of liabilities

Source: U.S. Department of Labor.

this month, and every month stretching out into the future. However,
notwithstanding this reality, as pension funds seek to optimize their returns, they have become quite attracted to the notion that they are single-
horizon, long-term investors. In theory, this fantasy notion of long-term
investing has allowed the pension fund investor the luxury of pretending
to ignore the consequences of having to sell equity assets to pay pensions
at the very moment when those assets are at a low value in the market.
Instead, for most pension funds, dealing with stock volatility has taken the
form of trying to offset declines in equities by holding assets that don't
tend to move down when stocks move down. Pension funds have tried to
do this by employing probability theory to predict which asset values will
move in which direction. This makes paying pension benefits more a roll
of the dice than an ironclad promise.

But regardless of how pension funds try to deal with stock market
volatility, the equity markets have been recipients of huge amounts of
excess pension fund cash flow as preparations for baby-boom retirements
have proceeded apace. If this trend continues, pension funds that should
be preparing to pay pensions with cash may end up having too many of
their assets tied up in common stocks. The implications of this trend could
mean steady downward pressure on the equity markets as pension funds
seek to convert assets to cash to pay pension benefits. It is hard to tell when
this sell-off might occur, and nobody knows what countervailing forces

might emerge to stabilize equity markets in the face of a sustained pension fund sell-off. Yet, it is possible that one of the principal forces propelling common stock prices ever higher over the last half century has been, at heart, demographic in nature. But, while it is impossible to predict the magnitude and timing of any potential pension fund stock sell-off, the implications of demographics for pension fund investors must not be ignored. Care and prudence must be the watchwords for every pension fund steward who seeks the historically higher returns offered by equities.

More importantly, stewards must prepare themselves to become systematic sellers of equities to reap the rewards from their stock portfolios in order to pay pension benefits. The financial objectives must be met. The lesson seems clear: Equities must eventually be harvested to help pay for pension benefits in a manner that conforms to the needs of each pension fund.

## THE EFFICIENT MARKETS HYPOTHESIS
## AND PASSIVE INVESTING

Complicating the equity investing behavior of the large pension funds is the disconcerting fact that most of the active money managers don't beat the market averages. This fact has often been associated with a view of the capital markets known as the *efficient markets hypothesis*. Sometimes, proponents of this hypothesis liken investing in the stock market to a random walk down Wall Street.

The underlying principle of the efficient markets hypothesis is that prices in liquid markets such as the New York Stock Exchange pretty much reflect the true value of those stocks, because all available knowledge about those stocks is in the hands of the buyers and sellers as they decide to buy and sell. As a consequence, the hypothesis goes, bad news is discounted quickly and good news assimilated just as fast. Money managers who select individual stocks because they believe them to be good investments do not talk much about the efficient markets hypothesis because it contends that all the energy and money spent in the quest for bargain-priced stocks is wasted. Discomforting reports that the majority of professional money managers fail to outperform the indices only seem to confirm the hypothesis.

It is interesting to contemplate the notion that the market *is* actually random in nature, either because of the efficient markets hypothesis, or for any other reason. Here's why. Let's assume that the largest component of a manager's investment performance is knowing whether, in general, the market will go up or down. This knowledge allows the manager to be more or less fully invested, depending on the coming swing in the market. Now, if market movements were truly random, let us ask the question: What is the probability that the direction of the market's movements is possible by sheer chance alone. Looking at a simplified example will clarify this problem. Let's ignore the magnitude of the market's movements and focus only on whether the market (however defined) is up or down at each year's end. If we make these admittedly simplistic assumptions and examine a seven-year period, what are the chances that an equity manager will have predicted each year's market movement accurately for all of the seven years? As it turns out, without the application of any skill whatsoever, the chance that a manager would predict the market seven years out of seven is about eight in a thousand. If there are 2,500 active equity managers in our example, about 20 of them would accurately predict the turns in the market for all seven years by simple chance alone. Granted the world is much more complex than this example, but the business of stock market prediction is nevertheless fraught with problems, regardless of whether the efficient markets hypothesis is true or not.

But, in fact, when examining the stock market, we can see at least two apparent trends that seem to dispute the efficient markets hypothesis. These are what are known as persistence and reversion to the mean. Now these sound like pretty fancy sounding concepts, but they really aren't very hard to understand. When the stock market moves up one day, it is more likely to move up the very next day. This is what is called persistence. When the stock market moves up sharply over one or more months, the following period will probably underperform the historic averages during the next period of comparable length. These types of observations are quantifiable and appear to contradict the random walk or efficient markets hypothesis.

Yet, these observable phenomena do not seem to be based on the utility values of equities grounded in the fundamentals surrounding each issuing company. Instead, these trends seem to be based on the psychology of crowd behavior, or what is sometimes referred to as investor sentiment. Is investor sentiment predictable? Nobody knows for sure, but to date it has not seemed to have yielded its secrets in a systematically predictable way.

But, that the efficient market hypothesis is almost certainly invalid in certain specific circumstances does not mean that it has had a negligible impact on the behavior of investors. One principal reaction of many investors has been to throw up their hands in dismay and not worry about the selection of specific stocks on the basis of fundamental value or the perception of future growth. As a result, many investors have turned to strategies that seek only to mirror the performance of an index and not rely on managers to exercise judgment in the more tedious process of selecting individual securities. This practice is known as *indexing*, or *passive management*, whereas managers who select specific securities are known as *active* managers.

Another even more compelling argument against much of the active management of equities is related to the fee structures for each activity. Passive management is less expensive than active management. There is strong empirical evidence that this factor, when applied across the universe of equity managers, will consistently favor passive management. As William F. Sharpe put it:

> Properly measured, the average actively managed dollar must underperform the average passively managed dollar, net of costs. Empirical analyses that appear to refute this principle are guilty of improper measurement. . . . [Yet] it is still possible for *some* active managers to beat their passive brethren, even after costs. Such management must, of course, manage a minority share of the actively managed dollars within the market in question. It is also possible for an investor (such as a pension fund) to choose a set of active managers that, collectively, provides a total return better than that of a passive alternative, even after costs.[4]

## SELL DISCIPLINES AND PASSIVE INVESTING

As practiced today, passive investors have difficulty applying a sell discipline to manage an indexed portfolio in service of any objective but mirroring the index. It seems obvious that realizing capital gains from equities requires that an investor sell securities. Active managers invariably design their portfolios with built-in rules intended to maximize realized gains or minimize realized losses. They say to themselves: "When the price of this

---

[4]William F. Sharpe, "The Arithmetic of Active Management," *Financial Analysts Journal*, January–February 1991, p. 8.

stock moves to this point, I will sell it because I have maximized my gain or minimized my loss.''

On the other hand, passive investors buy and sell stock only to mirror an index. In so doing, they do not exercise any judgment about how or when to sell stocks from their portfolio to generate capital gains. It therefore becomes the client's responsibility to decide when to sell out of an index fund. And, what's more, it is only by reducing an allocation to the indexed portfolio that gains can actually be realized.

The simplest example of a client-imposed sell discipline might occur as follows. On day one, suppose a pension fund decides to invest $100 million in an S&P 500 indexed portfolio. On day 30, the $100 million worth of stocks are now worth $103 million, and the pension fund tells its passive manager to reduce the pension fund's commitment to the indexed portfolio by the $3 million worth of gain. The index manager then sells all the stocks in the portfolio in a manner that allows him to remit the gain to the pension fund. At the end of the process, the index fund manager still seeks only to mirror the index and will continue to hold all the stocks in the same proportion as before the sale of $3 million of stocks took place. The only difference is that, instead of $103 million, the index fund now holds only $100 million.

Yet in the example shown above, it should be noted that reducing the level of commitment to an indexed portfolio is hard to accomplish without a firm grasp of our financial objective. After all, what purpose is served by taking $3 million out of the indexed portfolio? What will this money be used for? In the case of a pension fund, the reduction in commitment should be tied to a sell discipline focused on preparing to pay specific pension benefits during specified periods of time. So we must ask ourselves: Without a built-in sell discipline, how can we use equity indexing to help a pension fund move towards its objective of paying pensions?

There is a rational approach for pension funds to take to address the basic issues raised in this chapter. The historically higher returns available in the equity markets cannot be ignored. Still, board members ought to be wary of periods of possible separation between increases in the value of equities and the fundamental support for those increased values. There seems little doubt that cash-laden pension fund investors have put a lot of money into common stocks in the last few years, as they seek high-yielding and (apparently) highly liquid asset classes for their investments. In so doing, pension fund investors may be creating their own sense of equity value by having to invest large amounts of money in preparation for baby-boom related retirement demands. It is possible that this pattern of investing has placed upwards pressure on stock prices beyond the fundamental circumstances surrounding the companies whose shares are being purchased. Certainly, in the historic context of 10 percent returns, an expectation of 17 percent returns seems unsupportable over the long haul.

If the value of equities has increased for these reasons unrelated to the fundamental condition of the companies issuing shares, future equity returns may not meet even reach historic levels of total return. For now, however, it is hard to argue with the reality of the historically higher returns in equities when compared to fixed income. And, in deference to that reality, board members must seek those higher results, as long as they remain vigilant, watchful, and mindful that equities are a long-term asset class.

Yet, as pension fund board members seek to capture equity returns, in however careful a manner, it is becoming increasingly obvious that active management across an entire equity portfolio is probably not the way to do it. Nevertheless, by their very structure, index funds are not up to the task because they have no built-in mechanism to sell off assets and harvest equity gains in service of the financial objective of paying pensions. Instead, there must be a conscious decision on the part of pension fund stewards to manage the assets entrusted to them while being continually focused on paying pensions at the lowest cost and risk. It is with this thought that we turn to issues of asset allocation for defined benefit pension funds.

# CHAPTER 4

# PENSION FUNDS AND ASSET ALLOCATION

Asset allocation has long been a vital topic for pension fund board members. The reason it is so important is that far more of investment performance can be ascribed to asset allocation than to the selection of managers to invest those assets. Some studies indicate that asset allocation accounts for as much as 95 percent of the investment performance of a pension fund. Yet contemporary asset allocation is rarely designed to serve a pension fund's real financial objective of paying pensions affordably and without fail. In this regard, the topic of asset allocation has been left in the same vacuum as performance measurement. As we will discuss later in this chapter, historically, there have been a number of flawed attempts to allocate assets to meet pension liabilities. Most of these schemes were mechanistic and doomed to failure because of systemic problems. Yet it seems obvious that allocating assets with an eye towards the liabilities to be paid makes far more sense than allocating assets with sole reference to the historic patterns of investment return in the capital markets.

The examination of historic returns has its place, of course, but that place is subordinate to the greater task at hand. Nevertheless, today, most pension funds allocate assets with reference to a body of opinion known as modern portfolio theory. Modern portfolio theory is based on notions of probability and statistics. Its objective is to maximize investment returns relative to the market while decreasing the chance that those returns will be volatile. Diversification is an important central tenet of modern portfolio theory, as is the idea that past results, over the long haul, will point to future results. However, while these are important and useful notions, in and of itself, modern portfolio theory does not address the objective of a pension fund, which is to pay pensions. Accordingly, it is inappropriate to use modern portfolio theory as the proxy for a true investment objective when it is merely a tool.

Pension funds reflect demographic trends in society and our society is aging. As a result, many funds must soon begin paying increased pension benefits. All funds whose workforce demographics mirror those in society at large will have to do so at some point in the future. Pension liabilities are really pension benefits that have to be paid in cash someday. Younger pension plan participants have smaller claims on the fund's assets and payment of those claims falls many years into the future. Older participants have larger claims on fund assets and payment of those claims falls nearer to the present day. It is within this context that a reexamination of the commonly held notions of asset allocation must be made. We must begin by examination not only of the capital markets, but also of the pension fund's obligations and its funding structure to make sense of the job of allocating assets purposefully.

We recognize that the assertion of a connection between investment policy and the liability side of the balance sheet is heretical, to put it mildly. A prime example of the strength of the heresy is demonstrated by the fact that the most prominent modern portfolio theorists in the world, William F. Sharpe and Harry Markowitz, won the 1990 Nobel prize in economic science for their work, even though their theories are disconnected from any *nonrelative* financial objective. Yet we are not proposing that modern portfolio theory should be dismissed. Instead, we are calling for the subordination of the theory to the pension fund's greater financial objective of paying pensions. Acceptance of this approach will undoubtedly be received with skepticism among the sophisticates and academics of the financial world. Yet we believe common sense must ultimately win the day, regardless of the consternation that a commonsense approach might initially provoke.

## STEWARDSHIP AND MODERN PORTFOLIO THEORY

We have already seen how hurdle-rate planning and cash flow planning allow us to measure and consider investment alternatives with our true financial objectives clearly in mind. Once we understand our objectives, we can start down the road to understanding *applied* asset allocation. Applied asset allocation involves allocating assets to achieve a specific financial objective. In the case of a pension fund, applied asset allocation is the ongoing process of allocating assets in a way that provides the highest probability of paying current and future pension benefits.

Full consideration of these questions provides us with the proper framework within which we can address the allocation of pension assets to various investment areas. In this regard, the most fundamental question for pension fund board members is this: As pension fund board members, are we managing pension assets with the purpose of beating the market, or are we managing the assets with the purpose of meeting our obligations under the plan? To better understand our response to this question, let's return to some historic capital markets data.

## HISTORIC ASSET-CLASS PERFORMANCE

Currently fashionable methods of asset allocation look at the universe of the capital markets and examine historic data as a starting point for looking at the prospects for future returns. For the purposes of our discussion, we will follow suit by revisiting some of the capital markets data extracted from research done by First Chicago Investment Advisors, Inc. (now Brinson Partners, Inc.) concerning historic rates of return in various asset classes.

**TABLE 4–1**
**Investable Capital Market Performance (12/31/59–12/31/87)**

| Asset Class | Annualized Return[1] | Standard Deviation[2] |
| --- | --- | --- |
| U.S. small cap equity | 11.2% | 22.9% |
| U.S. large cap equity | 8.9% | 16.6% |
| International equity | 12.6% | 16.5% |
| U.S. fixed income | 6.5% | 8.2% |
| Nondollar fixed income | 9.3% | 12.2% |
| T-bills | 6.3% | 1.4% |
| Real estate | 8.5% | 2.4% |
| Venture capital | 15.3% | 35.8% |
| Inflation | 5.0% | 1.8% |

1 Quarterly logarithmic returns, annualized.
2 Standard deviation of quarterly logarithmic returns, annualized.

## STANDARD DEVIATION AS A MEASURE OF RISK

Table 4–1 provides us with the introduction of an interesting concept, the currently fashionable use of standard deviation as a measure of risk. While a contrasting view of risk will be introduced later in the chapter entitled "Weighing Risk," we should first consider the concept of risk as currently conceived. To illustrate standard deviation, sometimes referred to as a measure of volatility, we first consider that all investments of a certain type (each referred to as an asset class) don't produce identical returns. Examining the results from any asset class, we will see that some investments produce higher returns compared to others in the class, and some produce lower returns. In statistical parlance, we examine the distribution of the returns from the chosen asset class to see how the returns compare to each other.

Modern statistical methods don't just examine a distribution of returns though. Instead, they examine what is called a probability distribution of returns. That is, statisticians look at a group of historic numbers, and if there are enough examples of those numbers, a judgment is made about the likelihood of future numbers to be distributed in the same way as past numbers. This is an exceedingly important point in understanding this concept of risk that uses standard deviation as a measurement of volatility.

Next, a statistician looks at the probability distribution to determine what proportion of the returns are unusually high, and what proportion are unusually low—that is, how widely dispersed are the high and low returns from the average of all the returns. The more dispersed the returns are, the greater the probability that future returns will be less certain. Standard deviation is a statistical tool used to measure dispersion. When an asset class has a high standard deviation of its returns, those returns are widely dispersed and said to be more volatile than returns that are less widely dispersed. That is, they can be either very high or very low compared to each other on average. Nevertheless—and this is an important point—investors never know whether more volatile returns will be higher or lower than the average at any point in time. They just know that the returns are less likely to be clustered around the average.

So-called modern portfolio theory is based on the assumption that an investor must be compensated for the uncertainty of return that accompanies the historic performance of certain types of asset classes. So far, so good, if we assume that examination of the past is a good way to prepare for the future. And, in fact, historical returns show that, over long periods of time, there is a pretty good probability that we are able to predict *average* future returns. But, notwithstanding the averages, a pension fund must structure its investments in order to meet obligations, not merely to beat the odds. And when asset allocation decisions are made without regard to the real needs of the pension fund, a critical step is being missed.

## ASSET-CLASS CORRELATION AND CROSS-CORRELATIONS

Asset-class correlation represents the degree to which the returns from various asset classes have tended to rise and fall together, or rise and fall at different times. This correlation between two asset classes is determined through statistical calculations of what is known as the covariance between two asset classes and divided by the standard deviations of those asset classes. This measures the statistical relationship between the two asset classes. A correlation of 11 percent, for example, as exists between stocks and long-term government bonds, shows that 11 percent of the time, these two types of assets have moved up or down in sympathy with each other. Modern portfolio theorists like to examine what is known as the cross-correlations between each asset class and each other asset class, comparing, for example, domestic small capitalization stocks to international fixed income to see whether they move up and down together or separately.

Measurement of asset-class cross-correlations is deemed important by many financial sophisticates because of the desire to construct a portfolio with lower overall volatility. If returns from different asset classes tend to rise and fall in concert with each other, returns from portfolios with those asset classes will tend to vary more, that is to say, to be more widely dispersed. If asset classes are not correlated, then they will tend to rise and fall at different times, and returns from portfolios with these asset classes will be less widely dispersed. Since modern portfolio theorists define *risk* as a high level of dispersion in historic returns, then a portfolio with low asset-class cross-correlation becomes less risky by definition. But, as we shall see later, volatility is only one part of the risk puzzle and not the most important part.

Of course, just because asset classes move in tandem with each other or move in opposite directions does not mean we can determine that those movements are in any way connected causally. That is, we cannot say that a change in one of the asset classes has any change in another asset class. We can make educated guesses, but nobody can determine causality with precision because, in the real world, it is so hard to isolate variables precisely.

But causality is generally not the main thrust of correlation analysis. Instead, the idea is to allocate assets so that the increases in certain asset classes can offset the decreases in other classes. This smooths out the expected return and, in the jargon of modern portfolio theory, will decrease risk as a result. Naturally, this type of statistical analysis can be interesting, and even useful, but only when applied in conjunction with a firm grounding in the reality of a specific pension fund's obligations.

## PENSION FUNDS ARE MULTIPLE-HORIZON INVESTORS

Pension fund professionals who apply modern portfolio theory to design pension portfolios are fond of stating that the pension fund is the ultimate long-term investor. Their reasoning depends on the assertion that all pension liabilities are long term, and a pension fund investor can therefore afford to have all of its assets invested long term, whatever that means. In truth, *long term* has never been fully defined by the pension fund investment professionals because nobody has bothered to integrate pension fund investment portfolios with pension fund benefit payments. So pension fund investment professionals have stumbled along in a disconnected way, not really knowing what their investment horizon is, or should be. Instead, they merely repeat their mantra, *"A pension fund is the ultimate long-term investor."* Let's examine what we mean by investment horizon.

A good example of a single-horizon investor is the person who is saving for a down payment on a house. He knows that he must realize the proceeds from his savings on a single, specific date when he closes on the purchase of a home. Clearly, a pension fund is not a single-horizon investor because the investments required to pay the pension benefits must have many maturity dates to serve the needs of people of widely varying ages. Virtually every time a pension benefit is paid, an investment of some sort must be sold to make the payment. Even if an investment was made for a few short days between the collection of a contribution and the payment of a benefit, it was made and was then realized. So, as plan participants age and retire, the investments made on their behalf must be sown and then reaped. Because plan participants come in all ages, their pension investments must be made up of many investment horizons, from the shortest of terms to the longest.

Accordingly, a pension fund is a multiple-horizon investor, because pension benefits must be planned for a continuum consisting of the short term, which converges with the medium term which converges in turn with the long term, all within the context of an unbroken chain of pension benefit payments. Some people are retired today, some will retire in a year or two, and still others will retire in 25 years or even longer. A pension fund cannot afford to consider itself as only a single-horizon, long-term investor when its true needs are so varied.

Putting all this together, modern portfolio theory provides us with an interesting study of the characteristics of various asset classes. But these characteristics tell us nothing about the needs of a specific pension fund. Each pension fund has its own benefits structure, its own demographic profile, its own set of unique risks, and its own board. Asset allocation in a vacuum is a useless exercise. Instead, each set of circumstances surrounding a pension fund must be studied in order to allocate assets in order to increase the probability of paying pensions.

**FIGURE 4-1**
**Realistic Asset Allocation**

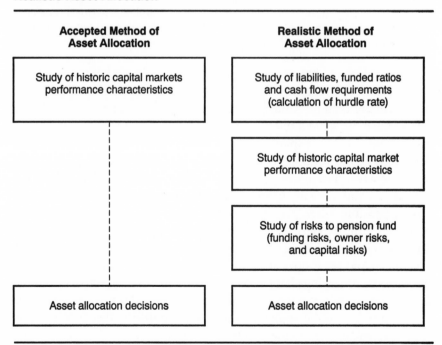

To illustrate, Figure 4–1 shows the accepted practice of asset allocation decision making on the left as compared to a more realistic practice on the right.

## MODERN PORTFOLIO THEORY ISN'T USELESS; IT'S JUST PLAIN AIMLESS

A short time ago, I was the chief investment officer of what is now a $24 billion pension fund. During my tenure, I had a chance to hear it all. The Wall Street investment bankers, the money managers, the academic experts, and the consultants all tried to ply me with their schemes and dreams. They would each invoke the gods of modern portfolio theory to bolster their sales pitches. The line would often go something like this:

> Hey, Clay, you will love our new approach to investing. Our historic back testing, when coupled with our current data analysis, indicates that we can expect to outperform the market with a standard deviation of 12.345678 percent. Think about what these noncorrelated results would do to your pension fund's total return, without increasing its risk in a statistically significant way. In your overall asset allocation plan, you should seriously consider this new approach to portfolio management, which is highly likely to increase your returns on a fully risk-adjusted basis.

I could go on, but maybe you have heard the pitch before. It always seems based on modern portfolio theory, which we examined briefly in the preceding section. Modern portfolio theory has numerous variations, but all have the same aimless logic. By aimless, we mean that it doesn't have an aim. Let us explain. We can all agree that a pension fund is an organized way to collect and invest money in order to provide people with pensions when they retire.

But in and of itself, modern portfolio theory has nothing to do with paying pensions when people retire. Nothing. This is why it is aimless; it has no aim. Modern portfolio theory uses statistical methods in an attempt to invest assets in a way that beats market performance with less volatility. And what does the single-minded goal of beating the market have to do with paying all the pensions? Nothing. The objective of beating the market is simply not sufficient to accomplish the task at hand. The central problem in the application of modern portfolio theory to pension fund investment management is this: Modern portfolio theory does not speak to the need of a pension fund to structure its investments in order to meet its obligations when those obligations must be met.

Modern portfolio theory does not take into account that pension fund investors must cash out their holdings by using invested assets to fund pension benefits as they fall due. Instead of focusing on paying benefits, modern portfolio theory is a perpetual search for the equivalent of the Holy Grail of investing. It is so involved with striving to beat the market that the true goal of the pension fund investment process is lost. Investing to fund pensions has a clearly defined aim. We know what our target is, and we shoot for it. Investing to beat the market doesn't even come close.

Modern portfolio theory's only aim is an attempt to beat the markets while managing volatility and asset-class cross correlation. But it is not totally useless: it is a tool. It has a use, much like tools have a use in building a house. If we look at a modern construction site, we can see that many of the tools have been improved over the years. The nail gun, the circular saw, and the electric drill are all enormously useful in the construction trade. But nobody would confuse these tools with the blue-prints. But if modern portfolio theory is merely a tool, why are we so quick to use it as the be-all and end-all of pension fund investing? Tools help those who manage assets on behalf of the fund execute the plan.

## PRIOR ATTEMPTS TO MANAGE ASSETS AND LIABILITIES

According to conventional wisdom, issues about the integration of asset management with liability management have long since been decided. The outcome has been deemed clear: Making connections between the assets and the liabilities of a pension fund is unworkable. Let's look at how attempts were made in the past to attack the problem.

The principal effort to match liabilities with assets revolved around what is known as a dedicated, or immunized, bond portfolio. Dedication attracted a following because it seemed to provide a way to meet pension obligations without fail, and to reduce the risk of not doing so. Essentially, a dedicated bond portfolio consisted of fixed-income securities purchased to match the cash flow requirements of the liability stream. That is, a bond portfolio would be designed to generate cash in a mirror image of the anticipated cash demands emerging from the maturing liability stream. While the design and execution of a dedicated portfolio could prove seemingly complex, the essential outcome was simple. If it was actuarially calculated that $5 million would be needed in a given quarter in the future, then cash flows from the interest and principal repayments from the bond portfolio would be designed to provide $5 million when the need arose.

However, instead of actually matching cash flows from interest and principal payments, many of those who chose a dedicated portfolio chose to do what is known as duration matching. The reason was that these investors believed they could enhance the returns of their dedicated portfolio by anticipating and taking advantage of changes in interest rates. While we won't delve deeply into duration matching here, it should be noted that this technique introduces a substantial amount of reinvestment risk into a portfolio designed for the safe payment of defined liabilities. Cash matching, on the other hand, as we will see later in this chapter, is a splendid way to pay your pension bills, even though it has largely gone out of style.

But if dedication is such a good way to pay pension benefits, why has it been largely abandoned? The answer revolves around several issues. First, there was a substantial problem with reinvestment risk resulting from having bonds whose eventual duration was shorter than the liabilities being covered. This duration mismatch can occur for several reasons. If the duration of the liabilities was forecasted improperly, for instance, the portfolio might mature before the money would have been required to pay pensions. More often, though, changes in market interest rates resulted in the dedicated bonds being repaid prior to maturity. Many corporate bonds are designed to be able to be called by the bond issuer for repayment before maturity. The main reason an issuer calls a bond is that interest rates have fallen below the original rate of interest being paid on the bond. In this event, the issuer wants to repay the outstanding bonds and reissue new bonds at a lower interest rate, and a bondholder must tender his bonds for repayment, whether he wants to or not. When bonds are called out of a dedicated portfolio, however, the bondholder is faced with the distasteful prospect of reinvesting the proceeds from the repaid bonds into other bonds with lower yields. This increases the cost of funding the pension plan and can necessitate an increase in contribution rates to offset the lower interest income.

The other principal reason that dedicated bond portfolios became unpopular is connected to the perceived inherent opportunity costs. That is, that given historic circumstances, construction of a dedicated bond portfolio requires a pension fund to accept the lower rates of return implicit in fixed-income investments as compared to portfolios with other, higher-yielding investments. These lower rates of return were perceived to have several problematic consequences. The first problem was the perception that contributions would have to be increased to make up for the lower returns. That is, the plan sponsor would have to pay for funding the gap between the returns of a dedicated portfolio and a portfolio that included nondedicated investments producing higher rates of return. The question became: Why should contributors pay for pension benefits out of their own pockets when pension benefits could be met from higher levels of investment income? A corollary problem was the persistence of long-term inflation that, at any level, gradually erodes a defined benefit, creating pressure on the plan sponsor to increase that benefit over time. It was reasoned that the returns from dedicated bond portfolios would lag behind inflation, and thereby reduce the ability of the pension plan to offer any cost-of-living increases in benefits.

It is essential to recall that past attempts to manage pension funds with dedicated techniques were aimed at dedicating most, if not all, of the pension portfolio. The problems associated with entirely dedicated portfolios are real. While these portfolios gave the plan sponsor a chance to match the flow of cash from the assets with the flow of cash requirements to pay liabilities, the returns inherent in the dedicated bond portfolio were low. Yet, by abandoning the idea of asset-liability integration, pension plan sponsors turned their backs on another reality. Common sense tells us that defined pension benefits must be paid. If we ignore our liabilities in making our investment plans, how can benefit payments be assured? This question has ben studiously ignored by all of the current pension experts. How can this be? How can today's pension funds remain indifferent to their obligations in the crafting of their investment policies? The answer may be a strange phenomenon known as invincible ignorance. Let's see how it works.

## INVINCIBLE IGNORANCE

When I was a kid in the fifth grade, I was a rock collector. I had a modest collection of this and that and wasn't really serious about any of my rocks except the fossils. These rocks had the power to keep me and my friends enthralled. Imagine, we used to think, millions of years ago an animal or a fish got caught in a certain set of conditions and over the aeons turned into stone. There was something almost mystical about the process. Even the names sounded mysterious and special. Fossils can do that to 10-year-old boys.

When an ancient fish died and was covered with a certain type of sediment, the minerals in the sediment would begin to displace the tissue of the fish. Gradually, the minerals became deposited in a shape that conformed exactly to the remains of the fish. When the sediment was covered with more sediment, the whole thing turned into stone. This process took an awfully long time, and the resulting fossils were difficult to find because they weren't out in the open. Instead, the fossil was trapped inside the sedimentary rock. You had to break open the rock to discover the fossil.

Modern fossils are no different. They, too, are difficult to find. Modern fossils are created when all the life and vibrancy is sucked out of an idea, leaving only a rigid convention. Fossilized ideas are concepts devised through applied reason that become accepted on faith alone. These ideas become surrounded with their own protocol and vocabulary and provide an established context within which people can interpret events and act according to their orthodox beliefs. The rule itself gives birth to conventions whose unquestioning acceptance can block understanding. This lack of understanding results in a state of invincible ignorance too profound to be easily overcome.

The process of establishing conventions is very important to the equilibrium of human thought. We have to categorize, to make rules, and to give structure to the way we interpret the world. There are many reasons for this. Primary among these is the human desire to manage and understand our environment. We do this through both reason and faith. Through reason, we try to establish what causes what. The reasoned approach helps us predict the consequences of our actions. Through faith, we reconcile ourselves with the infinite, with the enormity of the universe and our place in it. Reason alone leads to arrogance. Faith leads us to humility, allowing us to admit that we do not know everything. It is this humility that prevents the fossilization of thought. Consider the following story about how one powerful man was provoked into humility.

> Once there was a fool who set out for the king's palace. Along the way, people pointed and jeered at the fool. ''Why should a man like you be going to see the king?'' they laughed.

"Well, I'm going to be the king's teacher," answered the fool with great assurance. But his conviction only brought even greater laughter from the people along the path.

When the fool arrived at the palace, the king thought he would make short work and great jest of this man. So the king had the fool immediately brought to the royal court.

"Why do you dare to disturb the king?" demanded his majesty.

"I come to be the royal teacher," said the fool in a very matter-of-fact manner.

The king twisted with laughter. "How can you, a fool, teach me?"

"You see," said the fool, "already you ask me questions."

The court froze silent. The king gathered himself and stared at his ridiculous opponent. "You have offered me a clever response, but you have not answered my questions!"

"Only a fool has all the answers," came the reply, balanced on a sly smile.

"But, but," now the king was sputtering, "but what would others say if they knew the king had a fool for a teacher?"

"Better to have a fool for a teacher than a fool for a king," said the fool.

When he heard this, the king, who was not a bad man, confessed, "Now, I do feel like a fool."

"No," said the man across from him, "it is only a fool who has never felt like one."[1]

Matters of reason and faith must be balanced in application. To accept a reasoned idea in an unquestioning manner prevents understanding. To have faith in an idea without reason leads to feelings of helplessness and confusion. Everyone must seek this balance.

In upstate Pennsylvania, there are many dirt roads with deep ruts made by tire tracks. People sometimes say that we must choose our rut carefully because we are likely to be in it for the next 10 miles. I suppose these folks, spare and straight as poplars in their attitudes, are careful to mark the danger in becoming too comfortable with any single explanation of events, or way of doing things. They surely know that life "ain't linear and, as such, one size don't fit all." In plain talk, a person with a bad case of invincible ignorance is known upstate as a blockhead. I guess there is

[1]From *Jacob the Baker* by Noah benShea. Copyright © 1989 by Noah benShea. Reprinted by permission of Villard Books, a division of Random House, Inc.

a little of the blockhead in each one of us, but people in the institutional investment field seem to have more than their share of the problem.

A classic example of invincible ignorance is shown in the following story:

> For centuries, people believed that Aristotle was right when he said that the heavier an object, the faster it would fall to earth. Aristotle was regarded as the greatest thinker of all times and surely he could not be wrong. All it would have taken was for one brave person to take two objects, one heavy and one light, and drop them from a great height to see whether or not the heavier object landed first. But no one stepped forward until nearly 2,000 years after Aristotle's death. In 1589, Galileo summoned learned professors to the base of the leaning Tower of Pisa. Then he went to the top and pushed off a 10-pound and a 1-pound weight. Both landed at the same time. But the power of belief in the conventional wisdom was so strong that the professors denied what they had seen. They continued to say Aristotle was right.[2]

The institutional investment community operates as if the only purpose of a pension fund is to beat, or at least meet, the performance of indices. It's not hard to understand. Money managers can generally avoid being fired if they stay out of the fourth quartile. But the truth of the matter is a bit different. Beating or meeting indices is only a subset of the much more important problem of preparing to pay, and then actually paying, the pensions. This means that the challenge of beating an index must be made subordinate to the challenge of paying the pensions. It may be hard for money managers and consultants to understand, but (believe it or not) the purpose of the pension fund is to pay all pensions at the lowest cost and risk. A fixation with modern portfolio theory is fine, as long as it is made secondary to this more important objective.

Efforts to present these ideas in polite company have met with either blank stares or ridicule. Nobody wants to listen, it seems. The very notion of making a connection between the assets of a pension plan and the benefit payments that have to be made with those assets elicits only blank stares. It seems only simpletons and fools would continue to pursue this unpopular notion.

Nobody is immune from invincible ignorance. When the ideas in this book were first conceived, they seemed obvious—so obvious, in fact, that it appeared the ideas needed little explanation. This notion that our ideas

---

[2]Joe Taylor Ford, ed., *The Executive Speechwriter Newsletter* (St. Johnsbury, Vt., 1991).

were so completely unambiguous made us easy prey to the same invincible ignorance bedeviling others. Another important lesson about invincible ignorance is eloquently taught by Robert Frost in his poem, "Mending Wall":

> Before I built a wall I'd ask to know
> What I was walling in or walling out . . .[3]

Over time, the power of an idea is often undeniable. When modern portfolio theory was first put forth in the early 1950s, the reactions to it were mostly negative. Invincible ignorance reared its ugly head as new concepts were put forth and explained. Now, what was once revolutionary has become commonplace. Modern portfolio theory is not a bad idea. It is, instead, a very good idea when harnessed in service of a greater goal. But modern portfolio theory cannot stand alone. It must be connected to the idea of paying pensions. Let's put this important theory back into its proper place.

## SO WHAT'S THE GAME PLAN?

The baby-boom generation was taught by teachers who were at least in their 20s when they began teaching. Common sense tells us that teacher pension funds are therefore time-shifted 10 to 20 years or so closer to the present than many other pension funds. This makes teacher pension funds sort of like the proverbial canary in the coal mine. These funds will feel the effects of the baby-boom demographics before other pension funds.

As a prime example of this, today, there are approximately 290,000 members of the Pennsylvania Public School Employes' Retirement System. Of these, something over 90,000 are retired and 200,000 are working contributors. Over the next 10 years, the number of retirees will increase by about 5,000 per year, until almost half of the entire system's membership will be retired and drawing a pension. So, the system will go from 90,000 annuitants, to over 140,000 annuitants by the year 2000. In 1990, *The Wall Street Journal* reported that 50 percent of the teachers in New York State are already retired, with many more to come during the near future. While the teachers' pension funds are among the first to feel the pinch, the demographic circumstances of most mature pension funds are

---

[3]Robert Frost, *The Poetry of Robert Frost* (New York: Holt, Rinehart and Winston, 1962).

slowly changing, compelling them to face increasing numbers of annuitants relative to the number of contributors.

Teacher pension funds are a prime example of how American defined benefit pension funds are slowly shifting from *preparing* to pay increasing numbers of pensions to *actually* paying more pension benefits. Accordingly, it is becoming increasingly important to put together an approach to pension fund investing that is appropriate to this shifting challenge. To begin constructing a rational approach to this very real problem, we must begin by understanding the true nature of pension liabilities.

## LIABILITIES AND PENSION BENEFIT PAYMENTS

What does a liability have to do with actually paying pensions? A lot, as it turns out. A liability is a balance sheet term involving the obligation to pay someone at some future date from the date of the balance sheet. The size and timing of the promised payments compared to the ability to make those payments are the most important characteristics of any group of liabilities. In the case of a defined benefit pension fund, the liabilities consist of obligations to pay out pension benefits in a predetermined manner in accordance with the terms of the plan.

Thus, when the word *liabilities* is used to describe pension obligations, what we mean is the aggregated pension benefit payments made to annuitants over time. To plan a portfolio of investments to meet each payment making up this aggregated obligation requires knowledge of two critical elements, cash flows and funded ratios. And, as we will see below, neither of these two elements can be ignored in designing a defined benefit pension fund investment portfolio, or in judging its performance.

Assessments of both required cash flows and funded ratios are made by actuarial examination. This process of actuarial examination involves a thorough study of the demographics of the plan, and its historic retirement and mortality patterns. These are usually fairly well established, and don't tend to shift one way or the other. In contrast, assumptions dealing with future salary or benefit increases, as well as assumptions about future investment earnings, are sometimes difficult to agree on. Calculations stemming from these assumptions are particularly important because they form the basis for establishing the rate of contributions into the pension fund.

As previously discussed, if assumptions about salary increases are too low, or those about investment income too high, the pension fund will find itself having to raise future contributions to make up the difference, or eventually somebody's pension will either be cut, or not get paid at all. Alternatively, unrealistically high salary assumptions or unrealistically low investment income assumptions lead to an unnecessarily high level of contributions into the fund. The secret to successful pension fund management is in striking the right balance among these actuarial variables.

In this section, we will endeavor to show how to use the tools described throughout this book. As we have said before, though, one size definitely does not fit all. Each pension fund must develop its own plans and assess its own unique set of risks. Nevertheless, pension fund board members must remember the stark fact that while actuarial assumptions can be changed with the stroke of a pen, pensions have to be paid in hard, cold cash regardless of prior actuarial assumptions.

## PENSION FUNDS SEEN AS GROUPS OF INDIVIDUAL PARTICIPANTS

Pension fund liabilities stem from the individual circumstances of many plan participants. But it's hard to understand what is important by looking only at the aggregate liabilities of a particular pension fund. Because defined retirement benefits are a function of salary levels, years of service, and the age of the participants, we can use demographic information to better understand and categorize the nature of our liabilities. To simplify the process, let's begin by describing the needs of three very different pension fund participants, the 25-year-old, the 45-year-old, and the retired annuitant.

*The 25-Year-Old.* The 25-year-old participant in a defined benefit program makes contributions into the pension fund and has virtually no claim on these assets for some period of vesting time. Usually, that period is at least 10 years. Moreover, the 25-year-old has some 40 years to go before he or she is capable of receiving the full benefit offered by the plan. Clearly, this individual has little need for liquidity in the context of pension fund benefits.

*The 45-Year-Old.* The 45-year-old participant is in a different position from the younger participant. The 45-year-old has already become vested, and typically will have at least 15 years of service. This level of service represents a significant claim on the assets of the pension fund. Therefore, the pension fund is at a greater risk in terms of meeting the demands of the 45-year-old as opposed to the 25-year-old. What's more, the 45-year-old has only 20 years until he or she is able to reap the full benefits from the pension plan.

*The Annuitant.* The annuitant relies on timely payment of his or her benefit. If possible, the annuitant also wants the additional security of income growth to cover inflation. The pension fund cannot afford much risk in managing this person's pension.

By observing that pension fund liabilities are actually claims to benefits held by participants in the fund, we can begin to construct the integrated pension fund portfolio. But before we begin the work of describing the portfolio, let's review a few basics concerning the investment characteristics of equities versus fixed-income securities as those securities relate to pensions.

Let's recall the basic rules set forth previously:

1. One can be more certain of funding pension liabilities using current yields and principal repayments from high-quality, fixed-income securities than from dividends and capital gains on stocks. This is because dividends and capital gains on stocks are less certain at any moment in time than the income and principal repayment from high-quality, fixed-income securities.

2. Asset allocations to equities should be inversely proportionate to the need for cash to fund benefits of retiring members. That is, all other factors being equal, the greater the number of beneficiaries who are approaching retirement age, the lower the percentage of stocks one should have in a portfolio.

3. Asset allocations to fixed-income securities should be directly proportionate to the need for cash to fund benefits of retiring members. That is, all other factors being equal, the greater the number of beneficiaries who are approaching retirement age, the higher the percentage of fixed-income securities one should have in a portfolio.

Naturally, the examples of three pension fund participants shown above are grossly oversimplified to illustrate a conceptual framework.

And we have to remember that this viewpoint does not take an entire pension fund's assets in the aggregate. Instead, for the purposes of conceiving of this approach, we have to segregate the different ages of plan participants into groups, and then correlate those groups with the associated cash flow requirements related to each. Thus, any aggregate view of a pension fund will depend on the timing and size of claims that fund participants have on the fund's assets.

Thus, it becomes obvious to see that while younger plan participants must avail themselves of the historically higher returns available from equities, older plan participant must have the safety of high-quality, fixed-income securities to assure pension benefit payments. Overall, the emphasis is to take advantage of the inherent characteristics of *both* the pension fund demographics and the historic facts concerning the pattern of returns from equities and from fixed income.

Traditional methods of allocating assets attempt to improve the certainty of achieving the highest possible returns on an aggregate portfolio basis. Asset-class investment performance is considered only in relation to other asset classes, and not in relation to a broader investment objective such as paying pensions. Currently assets are allocated to improve investment returns over the long term, and to reduce the volatility in the portfolio through the minimization of correlation of returns among asset classes. But, however important the current scheme of asset allocation may be, we must not forget that it is a subset of the more important goal of pension fund asset allocation—to pay the pensions. Success in meeting this objective at the lowest cost and risk constitutes true pension fund performance. Hot pursuit of the maximization of returns without regard to the needs of the pension fund participants would be almost comical if the potential consequences of this activity were not so dire.

When looked at in a dispassionate fashion, common notions of asset allocation are inadequate to this task of funding pensions at the lowest overall cost and risk level. This is because these commonly held notions do not make the connection between the timing and size of a pension fund's liabilities and the vagaries of the capital markets.

A critical omission in the current pension fund asset allocation methods revolves around the size and timing of pension liabilities. This pattern of liabilities must serve as the single most important factor when allocating assets in a pension fund portfolio. Older participants in a pension fund have shorter-term needs that are not taken into account in the traditional asset allocation scheme. This is why a heavy allocation into equities is inappropriate for the retiree, but is perfectly sensible for a young adult. Similarly, while higher historic returns from equities are a necessary component of the 25-year-old's portfolio, cash and safer fixed-income securities are what the annuitant needs.

To illustrate, suppose a pension fund consists entirely of annuitants receiving pensions. If the fund is heavily invested in longer-term asset classes like common stocks, it is highly vulnerable to a bear market. If stocks are down and the pension fund is forced to incur losses to pay pensions, the safety of future benefits will be compromised, and the costs of funding those future benefits will increase. If, on the other hand, a portfolio consists entirely of working contributors, having all their assets tied up in fixed-income securities becomes overly expensive for the contributors and doesn't grow the plan assets in an optimal fashion.

Looking at asset allocation in the aggregate, without reference to the needs of the participants in the pension fund is sort of like a stock market investor looking at the Dow Jones average instead of looking at the prices of the specific stocks he owns. It may be an interesting exercise, but it doesn't have much to do with the investor unless his stocks mirror those in the Dow Jones. Even then, it says nothing about the investor's needs and objectives with the assets invested in those stocks. Breaking down a pension fund into cash flow specific groups of plan participants is the only way to connect the allocation of assets with a fund's need to pay pensions.

To properly integrate asset allocation with the size and timing of cash flows required to pay pensions, we must consider several important factors in great detail. Yet, without the proper conceptual framework, a true understanding of the process is obscured. This conceptual framework is derived by setting forth underlying principles of integrated pension fund management. Central to this effort are two concepts we have entitled equity importance and fixed-income importance. These concepts are described below.

## EQUITY IMPORTANCE

For illustration of an integrated vision of a defined benefit pension fund portfolio, we have decided to call the importance of equities in a portfolio equity importance, and the importance of fixed-income securities in a portfolio fixed-income importance. For the ease of this illustration, cash is considered a subset of fixed-income importance, even though it is a

**FIGURE 4–2**
**Equity Importance**

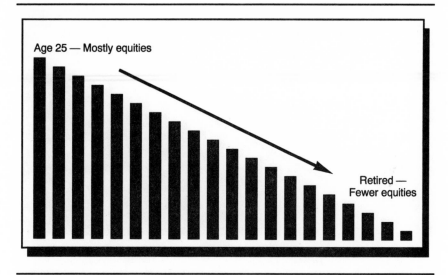

Age 25 — Mostly equities

Retired —
Fewer equities

special category to be discussed in greater length later. If we mentally divide the pension fund into separate accounts for each participant, we can see that for the 25-year-old, there can be a high degree of equity importance.

Illustrated in Figure 4–2 is the concept of equity importance in the context of an individual's career cycle as a participant in a defined benefit pension plan. Because a 25-year-old will not be vested and will have no claim on the assets of the pension fund for at least 5 to 10 years, one can afford to take more risk with this person's account. The 25-year-old can also afford to wait because the need for cash to fund this person's benefit is in the distant future. At retirement, though, there will still be a need for a residual amount of equities to fund possible cost-of-living adjustments to benefit payments.

## FIXED-INCOME IMPORTANCE

Now, for the annuitant who is on the other end of the age spectrum, there is a high need for fixed-income securities and cash equivalents in the

**FIGURE 4–3**
**Fixed-Income Importance**

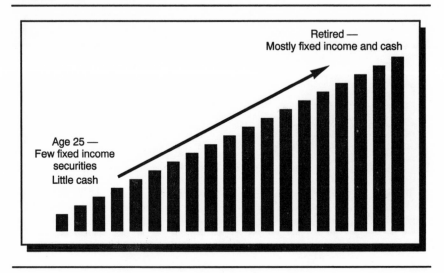

portfolio. Thus, Figure 4–3 shows an increasing level of fixed-income importance, as an individual approaches retirement.

## MOVING FROM THE THEORETICAL TO THE PRACTICAL

Now that the conceptual framework has been described, let's move on to the nitty-gritty work of building an integrated portfolio. The first and most important step is to have an actuary present demographic information showing the projected employment, retirement, and mortality patterns for our fund. This information is based on various assumptions that should be examined for reasonableness and then approved by the board members.

Next, the other, more difficult, assumptions must be set forth concerning likely levels of future pension benefits to be paid. This involves making assumptions about salary increases as well as other factors that effect changes in future pension benefit payments such as retroactive cost-of-living adjustments (COLAs) or health-care benefits. Remember that the primary base benefits need to be assured before anyone should talk about funding additional benefits. As with most actuarial calculations, all assumptions are interrelated with all the other assumptions. Changing one assumption changes all the others. The actuary must guide the board through this process, describing the specific alternatives in stark terms. The risks of taking one course as opposed to taking another course must be examined and understood. The consequences of each course of action must be considered carefully prior to making decisions.

Once the pension fund board members have agreed on a set of assumptions that give rise to a set of pension benefit payments that must be made in the future, consideration must turn to establishment of the contribution rate to fund those liabilities. This, too, is a difficult and challenging task involving the assumptions that have been previously agreed upon as well as a couple of others. The new assumptions involve the projected rate of return on the portfolio as well as the discount rate used in coming to the present value of the liabilities. Only by coming to grips with what future pension liabilities are estimated to be worth today can we compare the assets we have on hand to determine our funded ratio.

It should not be assumed from the cursory discussion above that this process is either easy or straightforward. The work is highly interrelated and can get complicated. The actuary and the board's professional staff and advisors must guide the board members, offering them assistance to improve their understanding of the trade-offs inherent in the process. Every effort must be made to construct a portfolio and then to monitor it carefully while disturbing the investments as little as possible. While there are notable exceptions, history has shown that neither market timing nor brilliant active management will consistently work better than a more passive approach aimed at compounding. Portfolio churning in search of ever-higher returns generally adds to transaction costs and the risk of error, but cannot be counted on to contribute meaningfully to returns over the long haul. Board members must remember to take a measured-steps approach throughout this planning effort. The general rule must be to plan carefully and extensively, and manage as little as possible.

## TOWARDS DEFINITION OF THE IDEAL PORTFOLIO STRUCTURE

Based on common sense as well as what has been observed in historic capital market patterns, in the ideal pension fund portfolio structure, equity and other high-return asset-class gains are harvested and the proceeds used to purchase fixed-income securities which, in turn, pay interest and principal, generating cash to pay pensions.

Naturally, this ideal flow of value from equities into cash would be impossible to achieve in reality because conversion of assets from long-term investments into short-term investments will never go quite as smoothly as one plans. It requires courage to sell equities when necessary to harvest capital gains to fund lower-yielding fixed-income products. There will be plenty of temptation to give in to the beguiling presentations of prospective money managers who claim to have a system to beat the equity markets, or predict interest rates. These difficulties make it especially important that the board establish its plan and stick to it, despite the enormous challenges in doing so. And, as noted previously, it is always possible that historic capital market trends might not continue into the future.

Development of a defined benefit pension fund portfolio involves applied asset allocation, which is the process of allocating assets to asset classes that provide the highest probability of funding current and future pension benefits. Each and every defined benefit pension fund must have three general categories of asset classes, all constructed in accordance with the intended point at which the investment will be converted into a pension benefit check to be mailed to an annuitant. These three generic categories are cash for the near term, fixed-income securities to generate the cash, and equities and other riskier asset classes for the longer term. Cash consists of cash and cash equivalents. Fixed income consists of those securities used for their ability to generate interest income and principal repayments. Equities consist of stocks and other long-term investments. None of these categories can be managed in isolation. Each must be coordinated with the others. We will begin with the cash component because pensions are paid in cash.

## THE CASH COMPONENT IN PENSION PORTFOLIOS

The cash component is the most important subset of any pension portfolio. It is from this component that pension benefits are actually paid. In the conceptual discussion above, cash is considered as a subset of fixed-income securities. In the construction of an actual portfolio, however, cash must be given a special level of attention and importance.

The funded ratio, contribution levels, and emerging near-term liabilities must all be reckoned with to develop the appropriate allocations to be made to cash. The plan actuary calculates net cash requirements for each period during the cash plan. This cash plan is developed in conjunction with the strategic plan both of which are used together to determine exact cash amounts needed to send checks to annuitants without resorting to increases in contributions or decreases in the funded status of the pension fund's balance sheet.

Under ideal conditions, except for an emergency reserve of cash, a pension fund should be able to generate virtually all of its cash needs from its fixed-income portfolio without buying and selling assets in an effort to control its cash position. Again, however, reality will dictate that the cash generation capabilities of a portfolio be monitored carefully to ensure all pensions get paid when they fall due. The use of a cash-coverage ratio becomes an important tool to measure the effectiveness of the cash plan. Pension fund board members must ensure that they receive accurate and timely reports of the cash-coverage ratio to tell how well their cash plan is working and to make changes in the plan as required.

The cash plan must be developed on a multiyear basis and reexamined from an actuarial and investment standpoint at least annually. This multiyear cash plan forms the basis for actually paying the pension benefits. It must be dovetailed into the plans for the fixed-income and equity portfolios. Because of demographics, during the 1990s and early 2000s, many pension funds will be moving into new territory with relation to the cash component of their portfolios. Due to these demographic changes, the cash component in mature defined benefit pension fund portfolios will assume a greater importance as pension benefits mature and become due and payable.

For years, most pension fund portfolios have been cash flow positive from contributions. That is, contributions alone have been greater than benefit payments. As a consequence, many board members have sought merely to optimize an overall portfolio return without any special regard for the timing and size of their liabilities. Cash to pay pensions has not been much of an issue. In fact, many pension plans have considered cash to be something of a nuisance. This attitude will change as demographic imperatives take hold. In fact, as noted earlier, it might be a good idea not to rely on contributions to generate the cash for benefit payments. This is due to the uncertainties surrounding contributions. For Employee Retirement Income Security Act (ERISA) plans, contributions could be jeopardized if the corporation falls on hard times, or has an unexpected shortfall. For public plans, budgetary difficulties may force a delay or reduction in contributions.

Management of cash will require pension funds to develop new skills. The crossover point will come when pension funds *must* turn to their portfolios to make pension payments. Pension funds that have prepared a well-constructed cash plan and strategic plan will have anticipated this crossover point. These plans will be prepared to meet the challenge of paying pensions using portfolio income instead of relying on contributions as they have in the past. After the crossover point is reached, funds that have not anticipated their cash requirements will be scrambling around trying to make ends meet, and open themselves to being whipsawed in the capital markets. These ill-prepared pension funds could end up facing the specter of higher contributions, lower pension benefits, lower funded ratios, or a combination of all three.

## THE FIXED-INCOME COMPONENT IN PENSION PORTFOLIOS

The fixed-income component of a pension fund portfolio is developed in accordance with the requirements to generate specific amounts of cash at specific points in time over a cash planning period. The process begins when an actuary helps the board define the set of planning assumptions. Armed with this information, the board makes a decision about how long the planning period will be, what fixed-income securities will be selected to feed cash throughout the period, and the risks inherent in each choice made.

Selection of a defined cash planning period is critical in determining the size and composition of the fixed-income portfolio. Only the board can define the cash planning period because only the board can make the decision about how safe or how risky the pension fund's portfolio is by its very design. We will explore the ramifications of the cash planning period at length later in the chapter, but, for now, let's assume the board has settled on a period. Once the length of the period has been established, the actuary develops the cash requirements based on the pattern of emerging liabilities during the planning period. Put another way, the fixed-income portfolio of the defined benefit pension plan has to dovetail into the cash plan, feeding it cash when and as necessary to meet the pension fund's need for cash.

Fixed-income securities are assessed for their ability to generate required interest income and principal repayments. The first step in this process would be to look at existing fixed-income holdings to determine which bonds can be used to pay pensions, and which ones are not needed and may therefore be sold out of the portfolio entirely. A certain level of fixed income must be determined to generate both sufficient cash to pay pensions within the planning period, as well as to generate some level of additional cash for emergencies and possible shortfalls. In many respects, this portion of the portfolio will look like the dedicated cash-matched bond portfolios abandoned several years ago. Yet it should be emphasized that only the portion of the overall pension fund portfolio needed to fund the cash requirements during the cash planning period will be dedicated, and *none* of it should be duration matched. The size of the dedicated bond portfolio in comparison to the size of the overall pension fund investment portfolio will be determined by the size and timing of the pension fund's liabilities, the funded ratio of the pension fund as calculated on a conservative basis, and the length of the planning period selected by the board.

There are a number of cash-matching strategies that could be used to meet pension liabilities as they need to be met during a cash planning period. But a simple strategy that minimizes reinvestment rate risk and provides the most cash coverage for the lowest amount of investment would appear the best choice. Let's see what this type of cash-matched portfolio would look like.

## BUILDING A CASH-MATCHED PORTFOLIO

The following illustration is purposefully simplistic to demonstrate the concept of cash matching. Assumptions for the construction of this portfolio include:

- A six-year cash planning period.
- A cash-coverage ratio of only 100 percent.
- Noncallable bonds with 10 percent coupons, with one bond maturing per year during each year of the six-year planning period.
- Level pension benefit payments made in the aggregate amount of $10 million for each of the six years in our cash planning period.
- Pension benefit payments to be made only once per year at the end of each year.
- We start our illustration on day one of the first year, and end it on the last day of the last year.

With these assumptions in mind, we start by assembling a portfolio of 10 percent bonds whose principal payment plus interest at the end of

**TABLE 4–2**
**Simplified Cash-Matching Example**

| Bond Group | Year 1 | Year 2 | Year 3 | Year 4 | Year 5 | Year 6 |
|---|---|---|---|---|---|---|
| Group six interest | $ 909,090 | $ 909,090 | $ 909,090 | $ 909,090 | $909,090 | $909,090 |
| Group five interest | 826,446 | 826,446 | 826,446 | 826,446 | 826,446 | |
| Group four interest | 751,315 | 751,315 | 751,315 | 751,315 | | |
| Group three interest | 683,013 | 683,013 | 683,013 | | | |
| Group two interest | 620,921 | 620,921 | | | | |
| Group one interest | 564,474 | | | | | |
| Total interest/ year | 4,355,259 | 3,790,785 | 3,169,864 | 2,486,851 | 1,735,536 | 909,090 |
| Group principal/ year | 5,644,741 | 6,209,215 | 6,830,136 | 7,513,149 | 8,264,464 | 9,090,910 |
| Liability per year | $10,000,000 | $10,000,000 | $10,000,000 | $10,000,000 | $10,000,000 | $10,000,000 |

the sixth year is determined to total $10 million. Let's call this portfolio *bond group six*. Next, we assemble another bond portfolio scheduled to mature at the end of the fifth year. Let's call this *bond group five*. In calculating how much principal we will need at the end of the fifth year, we must remember to account for the interest we will receive on bond group six during the fifth year, as well as account for the interest we will receive during the fifth year on bond group five itself. We then continue the process until we have our entire six portfolios of bonds assembled. The schedule of interest and principal cash flows is shown in Table 4–2.

Thus, as we can see in Table 4–2, if we add up the total principal (at par) of the bonds required to cash match $60 million of pension benefit payments, we find that we will only require $43,552,615 to cover ourselves during our six-year cash planning period. By adding up the total interest used to make the payments at the end of each year, we can see that we will have earned a total of $16,447,385 in interest during our planning period.

In real life, of course, Table 4–2 would be considerably more complex. The planning period will not remain static—instead, it will grow longer or shorter depending on board decisions. Most funds will want to have a cushion in the cash-matching plan, so they will have a higher than 100 percent cash coverage ratio as a result. This fact alone will introduce modest reinvestment rate risk into the cash plan, as any amounts in excess of the amounts needed to pay pensions will, by definition, have to be reinvested at unknown interest rates. Bonds will undoubtedly be purchased with higher or lower coupons than 10 percent, depending on market conditions. Most pension funds have to meet monthly pension benefit obligations, not annual obligations as shown in the example. The liabilities in most funds will not be constant for the entire cash planning period though we have selected $10 million per year in our illustration. Finally, a pension fund would constantly assess and reassess its cash-matched portfolio over time, to make sure it is performing as planned.

This cash-matched fixed-income portfolio is intended to take advantage of the safety and predictability inherent in high-quality debt obligations. The portfolio *is not* intended to provide capital gains from bond price movements. Therefore, there should be a minimization (or outright elimination) of the effort to trade fixed-income securities in the attempt to generate capital gains. Trading fixed-income securities in search of capital gains exposes the fixed-income buyer and seller to the profit-making prowess of the fixed-income trader. Fixed-income traders take advantage of the inefficiencies in the fixed-income markets, and returns are always impacted negatively as a result. As previously discussed, most fixed-income managers try to predict interest rate movements in one fashion or another. They develop intricate schemes to monitor the money supply and watch Federal Reserve policy with great care. Sometimes these methods seem to work, and sometimes they don't. Nevertheless, we must remember that fixed-income management is similar to equity management in one significant fashion; generally speaking, neither type of manager consistently beats the market. This has placed increased pressure on both types of active managers and fueled the demand for passive strategies. This is a cash-matched bond portfolio, and not an actively traded bond portfolio managed to maximize returns or minimize overall portfolio volatility.

## DEFINING THE IDEAL PENSION FUND FIXED-INCOME SECURITY

What kinds of bonds should we put into our cash-matched portfolio? Several features seem desirable:

1. The fixed income of choice must be of high quality. We are not going to pay benefits if the fixed-income securities don't pay

interest and principal on time. Governments and agency securities fit this bill well, even though many government fixed-income securities yield less than high-grade corporates.

2. Next, we would want to have steady, frequent cash flows. The regular need to pay monthly benefits require that we have frequent cash distributions coming from the fixed-income portfolio. (However unrealistic, in an ideal world, we would want a portfolio of bonds that generates *exactly* as much cash as we will need to pay each and every monthly pension benefit on time.)

3. If we could get it, we would like to have a positive spread to Treasuries of comparable maturities, without sacrificing credit quality. Naturally, we would also want to have a positive spread to the interest rate assumption inherent in the pension fund's actuarial projections for funding the liabilities as well as a positive spread to the hurdle rate. To achieve a certain amount of yield enhancement, provided one avoids the call features inherent in many corporate fixed-income securities, a portion of the portfolio may be placed in corporates as well as government and agency securities.

4. In addition to adequate and frequent cash flows, we need sufficient market liquidity to cover any unexpected cash generation needs.

5. Finally, the security must be available in appropriate maturities to be able to fund pension liabilities during the period of our cash planning.

6. Ideally, within the portfolio covering the first 100 percent of the cash-coverage ratio, the fixed-income securities should be noncallable, although from time to time this might not be possible if we are to obtain all the required characteristics.

The main point here is that the portfolio should be constructed of carefully selected fixed-income securities that produce the right cash flows to feed the cash requirements of the plan, including an emergency reserve. Many government and agency fixed-income securities will qualify under the above requirements because they can be made to pay pensions by their very nature. However, there is one special type of government agency fixed-income security that should be given a bit of extra consideration because of its unique characteristics. These are securities that, in the pension fund world, get no respect. But they should.

## MORTGAGE-BACKED SECURITIES

In today's capital markets, mortgage-backed securities could be a good potential fixed-income product to meet certain of the requirements outlined above. Mortgage-backed securities have high credit quality, monthly cash flows, a positive spread to Treasuries of between 90 basis points and 150 basis points, market liquidity, and sufficiently long maturities. This makes them ideally suited for funding pension benefits. Moreover, mortgage-backed securities represent one of the safest investments in the fixed-income market. People will pay their home mortgages because it represents one of the basic human needs: the need for shelter. And if that were not enough of an inducement, mortgage-backed securities are also considered a government agency security, with a certain level of federal guarantee backing up the payment of interest and principal.

It is interesting to note that, at this date, pension funds have not recognized the superiority of mortgage-backed securities in meeting pension fund benefit payments. Perhaps this is due to the possibility that pension fund investors appear to be afraid of the prepayment problems in home mortgages. That is, when interest rates fall significantly, many people refinance their mortgages, repaying an investor his principal at just the wrong time for the investor to reinvest the proceeds. As it turns out, the prepayment problem with mortgage-backed securities is compensated by means of the positive spread to Treasuries of comparable maturities enjoyed by these bonds. To some measure, this may be because not all mortgage holders behave rationally when it comes to refinancing their home mortgages, continuing to pay on a mortgage that could be refinanced to their advantage. Yet even this reinvestment rate risk can be minimized by proper funding of the cash planning period to a cash coverage ratio in excess of the anticipated liabilities. This emergency reserve gives the pension fund the opportunity to assure itself that it will have the cash required to pay pensions when due. And, given the higher yields inherent in mortage-backed securities, one strategy might be to construct your emergency reserve with these bonds.

In contrast to the problems inherent in the reinvestment rate risks of mortgage-backed securities, it should be noted that even a perfectly designed cash-matched portfolio of noncallable, high-grade government bonds with a 100 percent cash coverage ratio can have some reinvestment risks because of the timing differences between when interest is paid out and pensions have to be paid. That is, with semiannual interest payments on the bonds, and monthly pension benefit checks to be paid, there is a modest reinvestment risk that must be faced during the periods in between interest payments.

Regardless of whether a pension fund uses mortgage-backed securities, or solely uses other types of government or agency bonds, the idea is to have safety, predictability, cash-matched interest and principal payments, and a reserve for emergencies.

## THE EQUITY COMPONENT IN PENSION PORTFOLIOS

While the selection of the cash and fixed-income portfolios are of the most critical importance, once constructed, the balance of the pension fund's assets may be placed into longer term, more volatile, higher yielding investments. Collectively, for our purposes, these higher-yielding investments are being lumped together and labeled as the equity component of our portfolio, a generic term being applied to all long-term assets not placed into the cash or fixed-income categories. It should be noted that modern portfolio theory can be genuinely useful in managing a pension fund equity portfolio. Minimization of cross-correlation among the long-term asset classes, management of volatility, and seeking diversity are all among the legitimate objectives within this long-term segment of the portfolio. Use of modern portfolio theory in this manner could be called *applied* modern portfolio theory.

The objective of applied modern portfolio theory is to maximize investment values so that they may be consistently available to fund the purchase of bonds whose interest and principal are used to cash match liabilities as they fall due. The techniques of this discipline are well known to academicians and practitioners alike. Cross-correlation analysis, for example, can be used to compare different varieties of long-term asset classes to better ensure that not everything in our entire long-term portfolio is down in market value at the same time. It must be remembered, though, that while cash matching may free up assets to be invested in longer term asset classes, it does not eliminate, or even reduce, the need for vigilance, discipline, and prudence in making these longer-term investments.

With our bonds cash matched to the liabilities during our planning period, we could end up with virtually no need for bonds in our long-term portfolio. And, by using equity investments in this portfolio segment, we can overcome the previous objections to the use of dedicated bond portfolios. That is, we can have all the benefits of a dedicated portfolio within the larger context of a more diversified portfolio used to generate higher and riskier returns for the longer haul. Naturally, the proportions of an overall portfolio made up by equities versus fixed income depends on the liability circumstances of each fund itself. Yet, while the equity portfolio is an appropriate place to apply modern portfolio theory, board members must be careful not to replace a simple approach with an overly managed approach in their pursuit of diversification. Placing investments into conventional asset classes merely for the sake of having these asset classes covered does not necessarily serve the interests of the beneficiaries.

## THE SIMPLE APPROACH TO EQUITY INVESTING

The simple approach to equity investing places most of this category of assets into index funds that seek to mirror, but not exceed, the results of a given asset class. As previously mentioned, most active managers do not produce returns that consistently exceed the market averages. And, given that active managers are much more expensive than index funds, passive investing has the virtue of tracking the equity market at a low cost. But, there is an important difference between using index funds as a way to fund pension benefits, and using them merely because our active managers underperform the market.

For reasons of investment performance and its associated costs, boards may wish to invest by far the largest portion of their assets in passively managed equity accounts designed to minimize cross-correlations and maximize diversification. Any remaining balance of the long-term assets may be placed in a wide variety of investments. Selection of these securities will also depend on the funded ratio of the plan, the hurdle rate of the plan, and the cross correlations among past return distributions. These other investments may be actively managed as long as the expected returns, net of all management fees and transaction costs, remain consistently above the hurdle rate of return and above comparable other passive returns.

Even though, as currently employed today, indexed equity accounts, both domestic and international, have the virtue of being the best way to participate in the equity markets from a price-performance perspective, they offer no method for a pension fund to convert equity returns into cash to fund benefits. This type of asset conversion should be made subject to a well-thought-out sell discipline. But, the only way a sell discipline can be applied to an index fund is to increase or decrease an allocation of assets to the index. And, while today's index funds are open ended, pension funds have defined needs with periodic closed-end requirements. To address a pension fund's defined needs with indexing, there must be a way to integrate an investment in equities with a pension fund's cash and strategic plans. Fortunately, there is.

## ANNUAL PORTFOLIO REBALANCING

The objective of annual portfolio rebalancing is to reassess the cash planning period, reexamine the pattern of emerging liabilities, and then to harvest gains (hopefully not losses) from long-term investments to fund those liabilities. Accordingly, each year, when a pension fund rebalances its portfolio, it will reestablish its planning period and determine what proportion of the portfolio will be devoted to fixed income to generate cash during the planning period. The remainder is, by definition, placed into the long-term or equity category. Generally, this will mean that equities must be sold with the proceeds of the sale used to purchase fixed-income securities used, in turn, to pay pensions. That is, the allocation to the long-term equity portfolio should be increased or decreased in accordance with the need for fixed-income securities to generate cash to pay pensions.

This process of rebalancing emphasizes a very important feature of the cash-matched bond portfolio and its integration into the portfolio of longer term investments. This method of pension portfolio management frees the board to act and think in the best *long-term* interests of the plan participants. That is, once the board has cash matched during its planning period, the day-to-day pressure to beat the markets simply evaporates. Now the board can afford to take the long-term view because its obligations have been covered for the length of its planning period. When this happens, the board can focus on using the markets to pay the pensions. This means a board can lengthen the planning period when there are equity profits to be taken, and, if appropriate, allow the planning period to shorten through the passage of time when the equity markets are depressed. Contrast this, if you will, to the reactionary behavior of many pension fund investors when they sell into low-equity markets and buy when the market is at a high.

## DIVIDENDS AND CONTRIBUTIONS

Dividends from stocks should be reinvested back into the equity accounts because dividends are less predictable than cash-matched principal and interest from high-quality fixed-income securities. It is therefore harder to plan cash flows around dividends than it is around fixed-income cash flows.

Similarly, all or some of the contributions into the fund should be placed into the long-term equity category because we can never be sure when a contribution will be late or in a smaller amount than anticipated because of circumstances beyond the control of the plan sponsor. This will undoubtedly come as very unconventional advice to those boards accustomed to funding pension benefit payments from contributions. Yet when we consider the long-term demographic trends, future benefit payments are going to come from accumulated assets in a portfolio, so we'd better get used to the idea. And, consider the consequences to the pension fund of having to liquidate assets in a down market to make up for any shortfall in contributions. It just doesn't make any sense to rely solely on contributions to fund current pension benefit payment requirements. Furthermore, make no mistake about it, from time to time many public pension funds, and more than a few private funds, do not contribute obligated amounts into their pensions funds when promised. Today, this is a particularly acute problem in the public sector because of the generally poor financial condition of many states and municipalities.

Because the cash-matched portfolio will yield less than the long-term portfolio many boards may be tempted to make their cash-matched portfolio smaller than the benefit payouts, and rely on contributions to make up the difference. This decision should be made with reference to a number of factors, including the overall funded status of the plan, the size and timing of any major increases in benefit payouts, and the degree of confidence that contributions will be made in full and on time. This confidence in the regularity of contributions will differ from plan to plan, depending on the plan sponsor's financial condition and track record for meeting its obligations completely and in a timely manner.

In a municipality having financial difficulties, for example, a board may have little or no confidence that contributions will be made on time and in the amounts required to properly fund the plan. In this event, all contributions should probably go into the longer term portfolio, and current benefits be paid out of the cash-matched portfolio. Similarly, if a board decides that there is virtually no chance that contributions will be late or smaller than anticipated, perhaps only a portion of pension benefit payments would require funding from the cash-matched portfolio. But, and this is important, a board must not play Russian roulette with the pension benefit payments through an overreliance on contributions to fund current benefits. It is far better in this regard to err on the side of caution and fully fund the cash-matched portfolio than it would be to strive for that little bit of extra return that might accrue to the plan by having a larger number of dollars in long-term investments.

## THE EQUITY "SELL DISCIPLINE"

The sell discipline inherent in harvesting equities to feed the fixed-income portfolio must be made a structural part of pension portfolio management. That is, there must be rules governing the selling process. These rules must be centered around the need to adequately fund the required level of fixed income to generate the necessary cash flows to pay pensions. This primary consideration should drive equity sales. Moving in a descending order of attractiveness, the following rules apply to sales of equities:

1. The most attractive equity sale occurs when a pension fund is in the enviable position of selling equities at a profit that exceeds the hurdle rate of return on the portfolio, and is able to fund its fixed-income requirement with the gains alone, leaving the cost basis in the equity account to continue to build value.

2. The next most attractive equity sale occurs when made at a profit at or below the hurdle rate, but the fund is able to fund its fixed-income requirement with the gains alone, and can return the cost basis to the equity portfolio.

3. The next best condition of equity sales would be to sell equities at a profit that is at or above the hurdle rate, but to have to place part or all of the cost of the equities into funding the required allocation to fixed income. If the pension plan is adequately funded, this type of equity conversion may not be particularly harmful as it could represent the normal process of harvesting equity investments to fund the pension benefit payments. That is, if there are wide variations in the size and timing of a plan's liabilities, there will be periods when the plan will be liquidating assets to pay pension benefits in the normal course of events.

4. A less attractive type of equity sale occurs when made at a profit that is below the hurdle rate, and then place part or all of the cost of the equities into funding the required allocation to fixed income. Again, the circumstances of the fund itself may dictate this type of equity sale in the normal course of events, even though the funded ratio will decrease with each sale.

5. The least attractive alternative is to have to sell equities at a loss to convert the assets into fixed income to pay pensions. Selling equities at a loss will decrease the funded ratio. What's more, if this activity is done often enough, it will undermine the financial integrity of a pension fund, requiring increases in contributions, deceases in benefits, or both.

This final point raises a good question about selling equities in a bear market. What happens if a pension fund's liabilities require that the commitment to equities be reduced, and a bear market prevails during the rebalancing period? The answer to this question is not clear-cut because it depends on the circumstances surrounding the fund itself. The most important circumstance is the degree of conservatism used in calculation of a pension fund's funded ratio. If a pension fund has made imprudent actuarial assumptions, and its demographically driven liabilities leave it no choice but to sell in a bear equity market, its ability to pay future pensions may be dramatically impaired. This could occur because the pension fund loses the ability to recoup its losses in its equity account in time to benefit from positive compounding by harvesting accumulated gains. On the other hand, if the pension fund has planned prudently, selling equities into a bear market will not be as painful because its portfolio will not be relying so heavily on gains from the sold equities to pay pensions.

## ROAD SIGNS

So, how difficult is it to sell equities to meet a financial objective rather than selling equities in an effort to time the market? As it turns out, it is extremely difficult to make the decision to sell into a good market, or buy into a bad market. While the reasons for this are many and varied, many times we simply do not wish to take our profits in good markets because we want to believe that there are more profits yet to come. This is our greed at work, make no mistake about it. Our fear, on the other hand, works against us when we see the markets turning downward, and we try to stampede our way to the exits, along with everyone else. There is a way for us to avoid this behavior and act more responsibly. It involves being careful, patient, and observant of the road signs that can help guide us if we are willing to be guided. Naturally, if we choose to ignore the road signs, we have nobody but ourselves to blame.

In the book, *All I Really Need to Know I Learned in Kindergarten*, Robert Fulghum reflects on the common street sign, "Dead End," and recalls how people dealt with the sign in his neighborhood.

> Confronted by the sign "Street Ends," people drove down the street anyway. Not just part way, mind you . . . No, sir. They drove all the way down, right up to the sign, the big black one with stripes, the one that said, "Dead End."
>
> And they read that sign two or three times. As if they were foreigners and had to translate the English. They looked on either side of the sign to see if there was a way around it. Sometimes they sat there for two or three minutes adjusting their minds. Then they backed up and tried turning around as close to the sign as possible . . . Funny thing is that once they got turned around, they never drove away slow and thoughtful as if they learned something. No, they tore away at full throttle, as if fleeing evil . . . A psychiatrist friend tells us it's a sample of an unconscious need to deny—that everyone wants the road, or the way, to continue on instead of ending. So you drive as far as you can, even when you clearly read the sign. You want to think you are exempt, that it doesn't apply to you. But it does.[4]

## MARKET-RELATED ROAD SIGNS

The investment business has its own particular road signs that deal with market valuation. These are usually presented in chart or graph form and illustrate all manner of historic data. What these charts tell us about the stock market is that, over time, investors as a group have mixed feelings about the value of shares relative to standard and measurable road signs.

A dollar of earnings, for instance, is highly prized in one era, and sneered at in another. Thus, even if earnings were steady over time, stock prices would be volatile, just because investors are fickle about them. And

---

[4]From *All I Really Need to Know I Learned in Kindergarten* by Robert Fulghum. Copyright © 1986, 1989 by Robert Fulghum. Reprinted by permission of Villard Books, a division of Random House, Inc.

# FIGURE 4-4
## Example of a Stock Market Road Sign

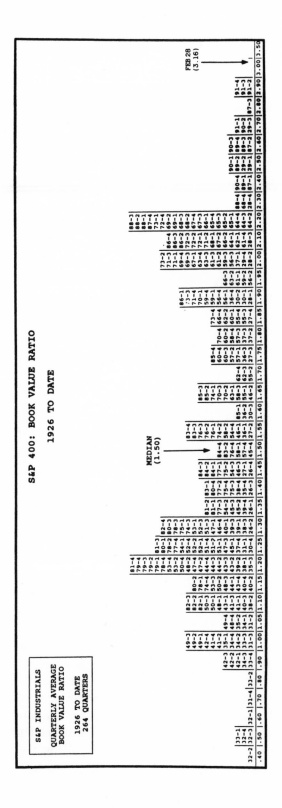

since earnings, cash flow and other indicators of financial performance fluctuate on their own, the marketplace for equities is bound to have considerable ups and downs. Stock prices get hit with both barrels: the natural ups and downs of company performance, and the greed and fear that characterize the investment community's behavior in general. Shown in Figure 4-4 is an example of a chart that can be used as a stock market road sign.

This and other similar charts are market road signs, and, as such, are unrelated to financial objectives such as paying the pension liabilities. Because market road signs are disconnected from a specific financial objective and therefore present only a narrow slice of the picture, they must be examined only in combination with other types of road signs to be truly useful to the pension fund investor. So let's take a look at two other road signs, a statistical sign and a demographic sign, to see if we can broaden our understanding by combining the different messages each has for us.

## STATISTICAL ROAD SIGNS

We have already discussed the concept of the standard deviation of returns. The standard deviation for equities gives us an idea of the extent to which stock prices fluctuate over periods of time. The important piece of information in this discussion is that, in the short run, the volatility of returns is at its highest, roughly twice as high as over the long term. In consecutive five-year periods since 1929, the standard deviation of returns ranged from a high of 47.1 percent in 1929 to 1933 to a low of 10.4 percent in 1964 to 1968. But, for the 198-year period from 1790 to 1988, the standard deviation was 19.6 percent and each 50-year period in that range was close to the norm. These types of statistical road signs are well documented and exist in abundance.

Yet we must remember that statistics, by their very nature, involve multiple trials and many, many data points in the effort to assess probabilities. This means that our use of statistical road signs must be tempered with patience and attention to our needs for asset conversions. If we have bought ourselves a sufficiently long cash-matched planning period, we can approach statistical road signs with the required patience. If our cash planning period is inappropriately funded, we will always be eager to react too quickly to statistics and not give ourselves enough time to respond with care and prudence.

## DEMOGRAPHIC ROAD SIGNS

As we have discussed, in the next few years many pension funds will need to convert equities into fixed income, and then convert fixed income into cash to meet benefit payouts. Retirement systems for teachers in the United States are a prime example. A great number of teachers will reach retirement age at the same time—within the next 5 to 10 years. This is a demographic fact, and a phenomenon that is certain and irreversible. These retirement plans will have to convert investment assets to cash to meet increasing payout requirements. Success in these asset conversions will depend on when the sales are made and how well they have been planned for.

If the stock market is bullish at the time of these liquidations, that is terrific for the retirement plans; but if the stock market is in one of its downward fluctuations at the time, then the ability of the plan to pay benefits could be impaired. Without a well-thought-out and adequately funded cash plan, this could mean that an expansion of equity investing could put both investment returns and the safety of principal into the sector of greatest risk at the very time that an assured source of funds is required.

Market volatility for equities—even over the long term—is high relative to other assets, but we can live with this because of the consistently higher returns equities provide. Statistical road signs tell us to invest heavily in equities, to capture high returns over the longer term, but the demographic road signs caution us to temper our judgment about heavy equity investing during the shorter run. The market road signs tell us about when the market appears out of whack with historical conditions, and paying attention to market signs enhances our decision-making abilities. In contrast, playing the stock market for short-term gain is just that—playing; it is reading the Dead End sign and thinking it does not apply to us.

## OPPORTUNISTIC EQUITY SALES

There is an opportunistic type of selling that can be especially attractive when the equity markets are at historic highs when compared to the various market road signs. Under many circumstances, this activity may be regarded as trying to time the market, a dubious business at best. But if a plan sponsor uses the proceeds from these sales to fund pension payouts, it is the need of the pension fund that drives the selling, and not solely the perception that the markets are overpriced. By funding pension payouts, we mean that a plan uses the proceeds from selling into an apparently overvalued market to buy bonds to generate cash to pay pensions. The reason this cannot be considered market timing is that it is the financial objective of the pension fund itself that generates the selling activity, and not the pursuit of an open-ended devotion to increased gains. What concern of ours should it be that the market continues to go up after we have decided to harvest some gains? Our profit-taking gives us the opportunity to lengthen our cash planning period, and enables us to act more deliberately in the future as a result.

With rare courage, it is even possible to accomplish this feat on an opportunistic basis in between rebalancing periods. The reason this activity takes courage is that the pension fund will be selling into a bull market, and nobody likes to think they have left money on the table. But again, this type of profit-taking is a good example of true stewardship, with the needs of the plan participants put first.

When talking about stewardship and money management, many trustees we have dealt with seem to understand the subjects on an intuitive level, but have a difficult time understanding what stewardship looks like in practice. When compared to stewardship in the abstract, it is much more interesting to look at what stewardship is when applied to a real-life situation. When trustees ask me what stewardship looks like, I am reminded of a story about Ben Shaver, the former executive director and current board member of the Maryland State Retirement System.

One day, during late August 1987, I was in my office at the Pennsylvania Public School Employees' Retirement System. I was working on a strategy to protect the system from the day in the not-too-distant future when the stock market's inflated values would make their inevitable drop to more reasonable levels. As I pondered this problem, the phone rang on my private line. Since few others had the number, I assumed one of the trustees had to speak to me. I picked up the phone, saying, "Clay Mansfield."

"Shaver here," was the reply.

"What's up, Ben?" I asked.

"I don't have a lot of time, and I need to ask you a few questions," he replied.

"Fire away," I said.

"What do you think of the equity market?" was his first question.

I replied without hesitation, "Overbought and overpriced by all reasonable measurement. It's not hard to see the evidence for this; look at the P/E ratios, price to book, price to yield, or any other benchmark. If I could, I'd sell in a heartbeat. Unfortunately, though, elements of my board think we are *under*weighted in equities, so I have to use cash equivalents and option hedging to lower my risk exposure."

We then talked about our respective portfolios and how much I would sell out of our equity protfolio if I could.

Ben responded with, "Hmmmm . . . OK, gotta go. I'm in a meeting. Thanks a lot."

At the time, I thought this an unremarkable phone call. Nevertheless, what followed that conversation was anything but ordinary. While I tried to protect the pension fund by increasing my levels of cash and hedge a bit against the impending market turbulence, Ben was doing something else. Late that August 1987, Ben Shaver was thinking about applied stewardship.

How was Ben Shaver going to react to the interrelated problem of having benefit payments to make in the light of what he saw was an overvalued stock market? Simple. He was going to take his gains from a bunch of his stocks and buy bonds. What effect did this move have on paying the pensions? Ben Shaver took his capital gains and was able to buy enough U.S. government bonds to fully fund the benefits of tens of thousands of annuitants for the rest of their lives.

To Ben, it seemed simple. By doing the right thing, he could assure that a large group of annuitants would never again have to worry about their pension payments. He believed stocks were overvalued from a historical perspective, and that bonds could be purchased and dedicated to paying off pensions. Ben made the obvious, but excruciatingly difficult, decision to act.

Defined benefit plans involve a contractual commitment between and among people. Simply put, this commitment is as follows: in accordance with the terms of the pension plan, contributions are to be collected and invested to pay guaranteed pension benefits.

How are these guaranteed benefits paid? Why, in cash, of course. And how does one generate steady cash flow in a pension fund portfolio? Not from dividends on stock, which average only about 3 percent to 4 percent per year. How about generating cash flow from selling stocks at high prices to take advantage of accumulated capital gains? This is possible only if you can muster an unusually high level of discipline to sell your stocks when the stock market is going great guns. If you have to pay specific pension liabilities, the only way to raise significant amounts of cash from equities is if the volatile equity markets happen to be favorable at the very moment when you need to fund benefits.

So equities aren't the answer to guaranteeing timely payment of pension benefits. However dull it seems, only by buying and holding debt instruments are we assured of being provided with meaningfully high levels of steady cash flow.

In many ways, the decision to sell equities into either a bear or a bull market depends on how well the pension plan has prepared to meet its obligations. If the pension fund is well prepared, it may not *have to* sell unless it can do so at a profit. If the fund is poorly prepared, it may have no *choice*. The well-prepared plan will take advantage of market opportunities to take profit in a disciplined way to better pay for pension benefits. The poorly prepared plan will have trouble selling equities except during a bear market when everyone else is also selling equities.

To better understand the risks involved in preparing well or poorly, let's look at the consequences of various courses of action.

## RISKS OF PLANNING POORLY

There are specific risks associated with the agreed-upon choices of a length for the cash planning period. If a cash planning period is too short, emerging liabilities may not be adequately described and planned for. If these cash needs are inadequately planned for, the consequences can be severe. These consequences are threefold, and may occur singly or in any combination, depending on the circumstances surrounding the pension plan:

1. Contributions may have to be increased to pay pensions. If there is not enough cash on hand to pay pensions, one way to generate additional cash is to increase contributions. As we have discussed,

however, contributions cannot always be increased on demand. If contributions cannot be increased to raise cash to pay pensions, then another consequence may come into play.

2. Assets may have to be sold at disadvantageous prices. Selling assets at prices that produce a rate of return lower than a pension plan's hurdle rate of return will drive the funded ratio down and place the burden of paying one generation's pensions onto the backs of the next generation. A similar consequence takes place if, for example, the planning period for calculation of the hurdle rate is extended to reduce the hurdle rate itself, in an attempt to portray the inopportune asset sales in a better light. Regardless of the assumptions concerning the planning period for the hurdle-rate calculations, however, it should be noted that demographically driven pension promises will not succumb to such chicanery. Pensions will have to be paid when due, regardless of planning that is either ill-conceived or undertaken dishonestly.

3. Pension benefits may have to be decreased. If the pension plan is not able to meet its requirements through increases in contributions or asset sales, there may be no other choice than to reduce or eliminate benefits. One particularly alarming trend, especially given the persistence of inflation, has been the establishment of two-tiered pension funds where older pension plan participants get more generous benefits than younger participants. Most often, a plan decides it cannot or will not support the level of contributions required to continue to fund a high level of benefits, and the plan sponsor forms a new plan that offers lower benefits to all new employees. In the future, however, we will see underfunded pension funds perform the same technique in an effort to get out from under the weight of poor planning and lack of foresight.

On the other hand, there are risks in erring on the other side of the cash and fixed-income planning period. When the cash planning period is lengthened inappropriately, the rate of return on the portfolio is sub-optimized, increasing the overall cost of funding. Put in another way, if too many assets are devoted to lower-yielding investments, more contributions will have to be made into the pension fund to fund benefits. Only the board can make these decisions, and mistakes should err on the conservative side, just in case. In all cases, though, the decisions should be made with specific reference to the liabilities that have to be funded, both present and future.

## THE DANGER ZONE

It should be remembered that the consequence of a loss is more severe when large obligations become nearer term. While this topic is explored at length in the chapter entitled "Weighing Risk," it should be noted that the choice of a short cash planning period can place pensions into a danger zone if larger numbers of people are retiring in the shorter term. This danger zone can become particularly hazardous if the pension fund is also underfunded when greater numbers of people are retiring in the shorter term. With larger numbers of retirees, a plan has fewer active participants to provide new contributions to make up for losses as well as eliminate the underfunded condition.

In this environment, it becomes even more difficult to raise contributions because each individual must pay more not only to overcome losses but also deal with the underfunding. If individual contributors cannot, or will not, contribute enough into the pension fund to move towards full funding, then the employer is left holding the bag. If the employer cannot, or will not, increase contributions to move towards full funding, then a future generation of retirees will probably see their pension benefits reduced.

## CASH FLOW PLANNING AND HURDLE RATES

As described in this chapter, the game plan for defined benefit pension funds has focused on building long-term value through equities and paying pension benefits with cash generated by a specially designed fixed-income portfolio. Given this focus, one might reasonably ask: If cash is so important, what do we need to calculate a hurdle rate of return for? The answer is twofold.

The hurdle rate of return is that rate of return on assets required to fully fund current and future pension obligations over a specified period. It is particularly useful in the management of an underfunded pension fund, but fully funded and overfunded plans will find it useful as well. The importance of the hurdle rate of return is as a balance sheet integration device. That is, the hurdle rate allows a plan sponsor to understand, at a glance, what overall portfolio rate of return on assets the plan has decided that it needs to meet its liabilities or obligations.

A hurdle rate also allows the pension fund to gauge the adequacy of capital market investment opportunities in helping the plan meet its investment objectives. That is, the hurdle rate acts as a sort of compass by which a plan can steer its investment policy and choose wisely among investment alternatives. A hurdle rate of return, in short, helps the pension fund board member understand whether the plan is gaining or losing in the fight to make progress in fulfilling its obligation to achieve full funding. If we focus only on cash flow, without regard to the funded status of the fund, we could correctly be criticized for selling off assets today that are needed to pay pensions tomorrow.

Calculation of a hurdle rate across the entire portfolio, both cash matched and long term, will tell the board what rate of return is required to attain, or maintain, a fully funded or target overfunded status. If the overall return on the portfolio lags the hurdle rate, the funded ratio will decline without an increase in contributions. The board must balance the need to strive for full funding with the need to assure that the cash-matched portfolio is adequately designed to weather any storm in the capital markets without having to sell long-term assets at low prices to fund benefit payments.

## SERIOUSLY UNDERFUNDED PENSION PLANS

Because the demographic imperatives for mature pension funds are only beginning to be felt, methods for dealing with seriously underfunded plans have not yet been at all refined. As a result, this topic will not be considered in the depth it deserves. Plans that find themselves in this fix usually have become de facto pay-as-you-go plans and are woefully unprepared to handle any large increases in emerging liabilities. Benefit payments from these plans more closely resemble payroll disbursements than pension fund disbursements.

In the context of this discussion, the degree of importance of striving to achieve the hurdle rate of return may vary according to circumstance. If a plan is seriously underfunded and its liabilities are becoming larger in the nearer term, striving to reach the hurdle rate may be exactly the wrong course of action, and could make the problem worse rather than better. Frequently, the response to this condition is to increase the allocation to equities, a potentially disastrous approach. If, for example, the plan is forced to sell off equities in a down market to make pension payments, they will lose ground with respect to their already sick funded ratio. The more appropriate response to this predicament is to acknowledge the seriousness of the problem, establish and fund a cash planning period, and then make the largest contributions possible into the long-term segment of the portfolio.

# CHAPTER 5

---

# WEIGHING RISK

---

## DEFINED BENEFIT PENSION FUND RISK

The pension fund that invests in stocks with short-term funds runs the distinct risk of having to convert to cash just when the market is in one of its inevitable—yet unpredictable—slumps. So how big of a risk is this? And what are its consequences? Before we get to some specific examples that illustrate this type of risk, let's step back and ask ourselves the basic question: What is risk for a pension fund investor?

It's a good question. In fact, the question is so good that it has stumped many an expert, academic, and money manager alike. Recently, while on a trip into upstate Pennsylvania to revisit my heritage, I thought I'd pose the question to the "men of roots" sitting across the pot-belly stove at Kirchers Korners.

"Gentlemen," I said, "how would you define risk?"

After a few awkward moments, Harold in the corner spoke up in disarming frankness. "Simple. I'd be glad to give back the cheese if I could get my head out of the trap."

Well, needless to say, this remark sparked a few-deep seated chuckles, including mine. Yet, the basic understanding of risk was definitely on the mark. And, as I walked away later, smiling and thinking about that humble view of risk, I concluded it must have been the result of the clean air of common sense. If we succumb to the allure of high returns that result in painful losses, we have engaged in risky behavior by definition.

So, what is risk? Well, armed with Harold's observation, it isn't merely an expression of volatility. No, risk is the function of the consequence of loss. Risk cannot be measured without understanding *what* it is that is being risked because it only has meaning when it is coupled with a consequence. For an investor, risk is the chance that, as a consequence of our investing behavior, we will not have enough cash to buy something important. For a pension fund, that something important is none other than the pension benefits themselves.

## THE OTHER FACE OF RISK

Over the past few decades, financial academics have developed a number of investment theories. One theory in particular has had tremendous impact on the world of investment management. This is the modern portfolio theory, with its use of statistical measures, such as volatility and beta, to evaluate risk in an investment portfolio.

While we have discussed volatility, we need to touch upon this thing called beta to understand the implications of modern portfolio theory as applied to pension fund investors. In equity investing, the concept known as beta compares, for any given time period, the percentage price changes of a specific stock to the percentage price changes in a whole group of stocks such as those that make up the S&P 500. A beta of one (1.0) implies that, on average, a 1 percent move in the S&P 500 will result in a 1 percent move in the stock in question. Beta does not measure mere volatility. Instead, it measures the tendency of a stock to move with the market, and not just how much variation could be expected in that movement. So, when financial practitioners and academics talk about beta, they sometimes refer to it as "market risk" or even "systematic risk." They then refer to those factors involved in moving the stock price that are not related to the moves in the S&P 500, as *nonmarket,* or *specific, risks.*

Specific risks, as defined in today's investment jargon, involve companies that perform poorly on a fundamental basis. Losses, slow sales, poor management, poor products, and too much debt are all examples of factors that contribute to nonmarket risk. The overall rise and fall of the stock market, however, is what is deemed to be market, or systematic, risk.

These theories of risk have found a place on Wall Street. Every portfolio manager worth his salt can talk alphas, betas, and risk-adjusted portfolios like the best of the business school professors. Pension fund board members, too, have been sold on this approach to the way risk is measured and dealt with. These developments are unfortunate, since the dominant view of risk has limited application to the management of retirement plans.

Robert H. Jeffrey has attempted to change the focus of risk as used in portfolio management practices. Mr. Jeffrey maintains that "the problem with equating portfolio risk solely to volatility of portfolio returns is simply that the proposition says nothing about what is being risked as the result of the volatility. Risk must be coupled with a consequence in order to have real meaning. And from the idea of beta, such meaning cannot be derived."[1] Mr. Jeffrey has touched upon the essence of the problem of risk and management of pension assets. Recognizing that risk must be coupled with a consequence gives the concept a broader meaning. In his opinion, risk is "the probability of not having sufficient cash with which to buy something important." For pension fund board members, who must keep an eye on both long-term opportunities and short-term cash requirements, annuitant benefits are what is at risk.

Mr. Jeffrey's ideas enlarge our understanding, but how shall they improve our practice? We have previously discussed the issue of actuarially integrated cash flow analysis and planning. Its purpose is to ensure that a pension fund will convert gains into fixed income, and fixed income into cash, and cash into pension benefit payments. Also discussed previously was the notion that applied modern portfolio theory should be made to serve the financial objectives of a pension fund in the long-term equity segment of the portfolio. These are adaptations of the academic theoretical concept of portfolio risk to the fiduciary's real task and deal head on with Mr. Jeffrey's observations.

## VOLATILITY IS AN ILLUSORY MEASURE OF RISK

When risk is equated with volatility, we lose an important dimension. Remember that statisticians measure volatility by looking at historic returns from various types of investments. Then they attempt to determine what proportion of the returns are unusually high and what proportion are unusually low. The more dispersed the returns are, the greater the probability that future returns will be less certain. Standard deviation is

---

[1]Robert H. Jeffrey, "A New Paradigm for Portfolio Risk," *Journal of Portfolio Management*, Fall 1984, p. 34.

a statistical tool used to measure dispersion. When an asset class has a high standard deviation of its returns, those returns are widely dispersed and said to be more volatile than returns that are less widely dispersed. That is, they can be either very high or very low compared to each other on average.

Volatility measures dispersions from the average. This measurement treats losses and gains in the same way, even though the consequences of losses are very different from the consequences of gains. Much is given to the discussion of gains. Virtually nothing is said about the effect of losses. Investments go both up and down, and the differences between gains and losses are important.

On the face of it, this difference is obvious. When we lose money in an investment, we have fewer resources to purchase what we need to buy. When we make money in an investment, we have more to spend than we started with. Nothing mysterious here. Yet, standard deviation in and of itself does not take this critical difference into account. Remember that risk is the function of the consequence of a loss. That is, risk is when, as a result of investment behavior, we become unable to pay for something important when the bills come due.

Only one side of risk involves the capital markets. To achieve meaning and relevance, we have to couple the risk of loss in the capital markets with a firm understanding of what is at risk in the pension plan itself. We must not become blinded by the illusion that the risks of the capital market, as measured by standard deviation, represent a solid view of the actual risk of loss in a pension fund. Instead, we have to view the losses that might stem from an investment in light of a pension fund's need to pay its liabilities.

Real risk can be defined as stemming from the consequences related to a loss. For a pension fund, true risk is measured by the effect produced by investment behavior on a plan's liquidity needs, funded ratio, and cost of funding.

## RISK AND THE CONSEQUENCE OF LOSS

Everyone in the investment business experiences an ongoing contest between himself and market averages. Current levels of market returns are the yardsticks against which the performance of money managers are measured, just as long-term historical market returns form the basis of their planning and expectations.

Researchers have compiled data that makes possible measurement of returns for different classes of securities for many time periods. Data going back to 1925 indicate, for instance, that domestic equities have given a bit more than 10 percent compound annual return—well ahead of domestic fixed-income securities at a historic rate of return of about 5 percent, both before inflation. These returns are, of course, statistical averages. And if the reader understands anything about averages, he knows that a man whose head is in the refrigerator and whose feet are in the oven is—on average—very comfortable.

Returns for shorter periods, quite naturally, deviate from the long-term figures. For the year 1989, for example, one measure of equities scored a whopping 31.7 percent gain in value, while socking investors for 25 to 45 percent losses in 1974. Thus, the general comfort of the long-term investor and the positive bias of the stock market conceal periods of exquisite euphoria and acute pain. That is an ugly truth about the stock market that poses a big problem for pension investors. They recognize the long-term benefit from owning stocks, but must manage in the face of sometimes violent deviations from the averages.

The superior performance of long-term stock investments would seem to dictate that pension managers allocate the bulk of their funds to equities. The fact that they do not is taken by some as evidence that pension managers are either weak-kneed or weak-minded. But, given today's demographic circumstances, almost all pension funds must plan well to meet their short- to intermediate-term obligations. They cannot just throw *all* their assets in stocks, turn out the lights, lock up the office, and come back in 30 years to reap the harvest that a positive bias in equities provides.

## AN EXERCISE IN RISK EVALUATION

To better understand pension fund risk, let's look at a hypothetical situation. Suppose that a defined benefit pension fund had no cash-matched bond portfolio whatsoever. Let's further suppose that we give a hypothetical equity manager $100 million to invest for five years. The five-year horizon was selected because of the real demographic trends evident in many school retirement plans, which point to an acceleration of normal retirements by the teachers of the baby-boom generation. This acceleration

**FIGURE 5–1**
**Assumed 10 Percent Hurdle Rate of Return**

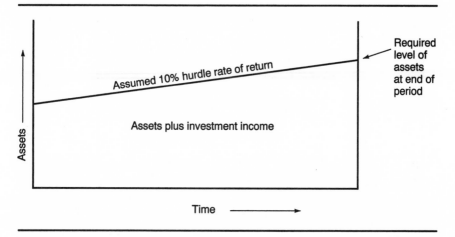

creates a more pressing need to get our hands on the assets in five years when we will need to convert equities into fixed income to pay out more in pension benefits.

We can further assume that we have determined our plan hurdle rate is 10 percent per year. As an estimated hurdle rate of return, and as a possible target in the capital markets, this 10 percent assumption seems reasonable. The assumed five-year horizon used in our example may or may not be the same as the termination horizon used to calculate our hurdle rate. But because the hurdle rate is defined as a constant target throughout a planning horizon, any shorter period within the horizon will have the same hurdle rate as the entire period. And, if our demographic trends point to an accelerated level of retirements in five years, it becomes important to stay on track and work towards full funding, regardless of what we have selected as our planning horizon.

By defining our problems in hard dollars, we can ask financial questions that bring focus and understanding to the consequence of a loss to our fund. This will give us a better view of risk as it applies to our fund's future needs. Our assumed 10 percent rate of return is shown in Figure 5–1.

Given our assumptions, let's consider what happens if the market plunges during the first of these five years, handing the hapless manager a 25 percent loss. It does happen! If he earned a representative dividend

**FIGURE 5–2**
**Recovering from a Loss**

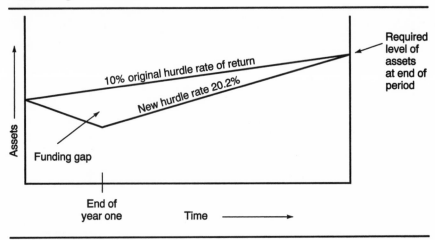

return, our manager begins the second year with $75 million of principal plus $3 million from dividends (for a total of $78 million). A little calculation tells us that in order to meet his five-year assets target (i.e., in the remaining four years) he must achieve an annual return of 20.2 percent.[2] With what we know about historical market returns, anyone who seriously bases the retirement funds of future recipients upon the expectation of 20.2 percent returns in each of four consecutive years is either irresponsible or a believer in some form of cosmic benevolence.

## AFTER TAKING A LARGE LOSS, WE MUST PLAY "CATCH-UP BALL"

This situation, which is illustrated in Figure 5–2, can be put in another way. How much "catch-up ball" must I play to get back to where I need to be, in order to meet the plan objective of full funding? Remember, we assumed that our hurdle rate was a 10 percent per year return, beginning from our original asset base.

---

[2]A 50 percent loss in the first year makes the catch-up game even more severe. In this event, the plan must achieve about a 36 percent compound return thereafter.

Faced with this new hurdle rate of return of 20.2 percent, the equity manager now has three options:

1. Invest more aggressively, by taking greater risks, in pursuit of the higher required return. (This is not unlike the unlucky gambler who doubles his bets on each hand in the vain hope of getting even.)
2. Pray for a four-year bull market.
3. Reject 20.2 percent as a will-of-the-wisp and ask the plan sponsor to pump more cash into the plan.

That little misstep in the first year has a tremendous consequence. Once mistakes have been made, the only responsible course for the plan sponsor is to assure that contractual obligations to pension participants will be met, even if it means increasing contributions. If the sponsor is a corporation, these contributions come from earnings—ultimately the shareholders. If the sponsor is a public body, the added funds must come from taxpayers' pockets. Unfortunately, given the constraints of the real world, the plan sponsor may simply *be unable* to act responsibly. This is the consequence that the board members must consider as they allocate funds, and it explains why pension funds with near-term payout requirements avoid large commitments to equities without first fully funding their cash-matched portfolio in the context of a well-thought-out cash plan.

Now, modern portfolio theorists will surely assert that they would never be left so exposed to market volatility. Instead, through the minimization of cross-correlations among asset classes, they believe they can avoid these large swings in portfolio value. And, to some degree, these techniques work as advertised, when viewed from a statistical perspective, on average. Yet, why would we want to subject pension fund contributors and plan participants to the chance that statistical anomalies will hurt our plan's ability to pay pensions while maintaining our target-funded ratio? It seems a far wiser course to fully plan and properly fund a cash-matched planning period that allows the pension fund to ride out any storm in the markets. In this way, gains harvested from the market's higher periods are put in deliberate service of meeting the financial objective of paying the pensions at the lowest cost to the contributors, and the lowest risk of nonpayment of pension benefits to the plan participants.

## A SIMPLE WAY TO CALCULATE PENSION FUND RISK

It may be useful to think about the entire job of striving for full funding as having to earn a certain required rate of return during a specified period of time. It may also be handy to think of the required rate of return in the form shown below. A fund's starting asset base is multiplied by the numbers shown below, in order to see what the value of those assets will be when they are compounded at 10 percent per year for each of five years. The 10 percent number is selected as an example, and the required rate of return for any given fund will be different because each situation is unique. What we get when we multiply the two numbers together is the result of that year's compounding. Remember that compounding produces returns on the previous year's asset base, which includes earnings on the previous years' returns.

| | |
|---|---|
| Start | 1.00 X Starting asset base |
| End year 1 | 1.10 X Starting asset base |
| End year 2 | 1.21 X Starting asset base |
| End year 3 | 1.33 X Starting asset base |
| End year 4 | 1.46 X Starting asset base |
| End year 5 | 1.60 X Starting asset base |

So, in the fourth year of our example above, we see that we would need an additional 46 cents for each dollar of starting asset base in order to have grown that starting asset base by 10 percent per year for four years.

Now, back to risk. By its nature, risk involves the problems brought about through loss of pension fund money during the time we need to achieve full funding. Let's look at our original example. To calculate the return required to adjust for a 25 percent loss at the end of the first year and also the return required to make up for the originally planned 10 percent growth in assets, we can use an easy trial-and-error method. In order to simplify the task, we have selected three sample returns to test out the effects of our hypothetical loss: a 10 percent return, a 20 percent return, or a 25 percent return.

The point of the exercise is to come as close as possible, through trial and error, in calculating the amount needed to recoup our losses, get back to parity, and again earn the rate of return needed to become fully funded. Put another way, if we first try a 10 percent return on all of our assets after a 25 percent loss in the first year, how far will we be towards our goal of full funding? Next, we try a 20 percent return to see how well that moves us towards our objective. Finally, we try a 25 percent return and see what that does. When we compare each result from our trial-and-error process to our requirements, we can estimate how much higher a return is necessary to get back on track.

Here's an easy way to play this game for yourself, thought up by my friend Ben Shaver, the former executive director of the Maryland State Retirement System. You play it by using a #2 pencil as a sophisticated financial calculator. This is called:

**Uncle Ben's Ticonderoga #2 Risk Calculator**

|  | 10% | 20% | 25% |
|---|---|---|---|
| End year 1 | .75X | .75X | .75X |
| End year 2 | .825 | .90 | .9375 |
| End year 3 | .9075 | 1.08 | 1.1699 |
| End year 4 | .99825 | 1.296 | 1.4624 |
| End year 5 | 1.0807 | 1.552 | 1.82 |

So, according to our first chart, if we had a 10 percent hurdle rate to move us toward full funding, then at the end of the fifth year, we would need to have earned an additional 60 cents for every dollar we started with. If we look at Uncle Ben's calculator, after a 25 percent loss in the first year, a 10 percent per year rate of return would give us only about eight cents for every original dollar (see the 1.0807 multiplier above). To get close to the additional 60 cents that we need, we would have to earn somewhere between 20 percent per year (which would earn us about 55.2 cents on every original dollar), and 25 percent per year (which would get us about 82 cents).

So we need a lot of earnings to make up for one little 25 percent mistake, huh? And, in point of fact, it is possible, over time, to earn and compound our way out of our losses. But, if we have large looming liabilities working against us, time is our enemy, not our friend. In this position, we cannot afford to sit back and let time work for us because it won't. This is why we must buy ourselves the time to allow for the recovery from losses by fully funding a well-planned cash-matched portfolio to cover our plan participants while we wait for more positive events to unfold.

## THE FIRST RESPONSIBILITY OF PENSION FUND BOARD MEMBERS

Unlike that of other investors, the first responsibility of defined benefit pension fund board members is to meet contractual benefit payments;

maximizing returns comes later in the pecking order. Their duty of stewardship requires that they give up some of the attractive averages of stocks for the greater certainty of less rewarding investments. These less rewarding investments are in our cash-matched bond portfolio, and are used to assure ourselves of the ability to pay pensions.

Remember that actuarial risks relate benefits (liabilities) to assets and cash flow, and to the time (investment horizon) available to meet them. Taken in and of itself, volatility does not relate to a pension fund's liabilities. Additionally, and equally important, the actuarial form of approaching risk lets us derive hurdle rates that enable us to be more discrete and more selective in our approach to the capital markets. Interestingly, when one is investing in order to provide funding for well-defined obligations, there is an ability to plan out how to make fewer mistakes. Volatility does not permit that capability because it is unrelated to anything but market performance.

## THE POWER OF COMPOUNDING

We all have heard of the power of compound interest. If we compound $15,000 at 10 percent per year for 25 years, we will have $162,521 at the end of the period. Compounding interest is a slow, sure, simple way of increasing resources over time. But when we introduce the concepts of time and compounding into our discussion of risk, we enter into uncharted waters. Like gains, losses also have a compounding effect that is dependent on time for its magnitude. This effect works in a reverse fashion over time when compared to the compounding effect of gains. The effect of compound losses depends on the timing of the liabilities to be paid from the portfolio of investments.

The severity of a loss is compounded to a greater degree as the liability to be paid moves closer to the present. If I have $100 today, and need to pay a liability of $100 next week, I'd better not lose any money between now and then. If I have $100 today and have to pay a liability of $100 five years from today, I have more time to recover from any losses I might incur between today and five years from today. This means that as our investment time horizon contracts, we cannot afford to reach for extra yield because we don't have the time available to recover from a possible loss. This seems counterintuitive, but the impact of a loss is more keenly felt when we have near-term liabilities.

Unfortunately, even though capital market conditions are only one piece to the risk puzzle, conventional pension risk management practices deal *only* with capital market conditions. This orientation is gravely flawed. Instead, prudent risk assessment must rely on a dispassionate consideration of the timing and size of the liabilities to be paid and then look at what is available in the capital markets to pay those liabilities.

When the time horizon of liability payments allows a more tolerant view of the risk of loss, we can afford to invest in riskier investments because we have enough time to recover from any losses that may occur. As liabilities move closer to the present, though, taking such risks becomes less acceptable. The critical component in risk analysis is in striving to achieve the proper balance between the imperatives derived from a pension fund's balance sheet and conditions in the capital markets.

When capital market conditions do not allow us to earn our hurdle rate, many investors are tempted to reach for that little bit of extra yield to try to bridge the gap. This reaching for extra return increases the risk of loss, especially when liabilities must be paid within the near term. The magnitude of the risk is determined by the time horizon remaining to recover from the loss. If we have a sufficiently long horizon, the consequences arising from the risk of loss can be minimal. If our liabilities force us to have a shorter time horizon, however, the risk arising from a loss increases dramatically.

Remember, an increased exposure to risk does not ensure higher returns. Increased risk puts us into the arena of higher losses as well as higher gains. These losses become more financially important as our liability payments grow larger and nearer in time to the present. During a period of losses, without an increase in contributions, larger liability payments may force us to sell, driving our funded ratio down. Ironically, instead of having made the situation better through reaching for a higher, riskier return, we may make things worse. If we incur losses when there are large, near-term liabilities to pay, contributions into the pension fund will have to be increased to prevent a decline in funded status.

It is possible to reach for higher, riskier returns if our liability structure permits, but the attitude that the acceptance of higher risk inevitably leads to higher returns ignores reality. The illusion that risk is properly and completely measured by standard deviation overlooks the consequences of loss stemming from an investment time horizon and the status of liabilities. Standard deviation is an incomplete proxy for risk measurement. Once again, a tool of modern portfolio theory shows itself to be unconnected from the true purpose of pension fund investment management.

## LIMITATIONS TO ALL COMMERCIAL ACTIVITY

In virtually all aspects of the commercial world, there are boundaries constraining the behavior of buyers and sellers. The fundamental measurement of a commercial boundary line is the price that a willing buyer and seller agree upon in a transaction. In practice, this boundary line is more like a range than a line, but that range is not without limits.

The stock market world is not exempt from the rules of commercial behavior. The ranges of high and low acceptable prices for stocks vary from time to time, but annualized returns have averaged around 10 percent over the last 65 years or so. During the decade of the 1980s, annualized returns were a little less than 17 percent.

Can anyone doubt that trees don't grow to the sky and stock prices don't go up forever? There are limits, after all, despite wishful thinkers who would argue otherwise. Pension fund board members would do well to realize that stock prices do have limits, and not get caught up in wishful thinking that they don't. Board members must be aware of this reality. To do so is to be forewarned against the inevitable elevator free-fall of stock prices endemic to modern institutional markets. Consider the following little story and see if we cannot recognize a little bit of all of us in the characters:

> A couple of hunters chartered a plane to fly them into a forest territory. Two weeks later, the pilot came to take them back. He took a look at the animals they had shot and said, "This plane won't take more than one buffalo. You'll have to leave the other behind."
>
> "But the last time, the pilot let us take two in a plane this size," the hunters protested.
>
> The pilot was doubtful, but finally said, "Well, if you did it last time, I guess we can do it again." So the plane took off with the three men and two buffaloes. But it couldn't gain height and crashed into a neighboring hill.
>
> The men climbed out and looked around. One hunter said to the other, "Where do you think we are?"
>
> The other inspected the surroundings and said, "I think we're about two miles to the right of where we crashed last time."[3]

---

[3]Anthony de Mello, *Taking Flight* (New York: Doubleday Publishing, 1988).

## THE INSANITY OF CONCEIT

All too often, though, when it comes to matters of risk, we tend to believe the worst cannot happen. Our ability to deal with the problem of the risk of loss arises from many conditions. One such condition is related to the tendency we all have to believe that we are less likely to encounter misfortune than is the other guy. Perhaps this perspective is derived from an all-too-common tendency to seek out information that confirms what we want to believe, rather than to consider elements of the problem that run contrary to our beliefs. Regardless, when it comes to matters of weighing risk, we all tend to fall prey to what can be characterized as the "insanity of conceit." The insanity of conceit is an equal opportunity disease. Its origins date from man's first existence. The afflicted exhibits the following symptoms:

1. He hears, but doesn't listen.
2. He fails to see the obvious or understand its meaning.
3. When history is on the verge of repeating itself, he proclaims that *this time it's different!*

To illustrate, consider the craps player in a casino. He knows the entire casino is built on gambling losses. He knows that the pretty waitresses, sumptuous carpets, cheap meals, and flashy entertainment are all paid for by people like himself. Yet, he plays his heart out in the belief that he can beat the house. Have you ever watched how these folks play the table? They start out slowly, with two buck bets. They win a little, and they lose a little. Then they happen to have a few lucky rolls and believe they are on a hot streak. Of course, the pit boss knows that the house will always win in the long run. And even the gambler knows that the odds are against him. But the allure of the moment, the intoxication of the dice, whispers to his heart, "You're on a hot streak! Go, baby go!" To make matters worse, now there's a small crowd of people behind the shooter, urging him on, feeding on the excitement.

In some corner of his mind, the gambler knows he can lose it all with a single throw of the dice. But the dollars begin to rise, and he feels invulnerable. First it's $100, then $200, then $500. He is invincible. Nothing can touch him now. The hot hand and the crowd both attest to the fact that he is special; that he is exempt from the laws of chance. But, even while the gambler continues to win, the pit boss smiles. The boss knows how the casino makes money, and that the odds are with the house.

The whole system is rigged so that even if this shooter makes off with a couple of thousand dollars, there will be many more shooters who will lose it all on the next throw. And that's just what happens. Old snake eyes rears his ugly head at last, and the streak is over. The crowd groans, and then disperses. The gambler sighs and thinks he almost had it all. And yet, despite his loss, he remains blind to the facts of the game. He just knows that Lady Luck is smiling down on him, and, as he strolls back to the table, *this time things will be different.*

Ladies and gentlemen, what we see here is the insanity of conceit. The insanity of conceit is pride, intellectual or otherwise. In the above illustration, we were dealing with a gambler. Gambling is an easy target for demonstrating the problem. But the insanity of conceit shows up everywhere. It happens when a consultant relies on an outmoded theory as an underpinning for his advice. It happens when a money manager feels he can do no wrong, and keeps playing the game when he should be sitting on the sidelines. And it happens in a pension fund, where a board refuses to admit that yesterday's answers are not always right for today's problems. Board members must be able to recognize and deal with its constant, alluring persuasiveness, especially in matters in which pension assets are being placed at a risk of loss. In our roles as stewards, we cannot afford to give in to this affliction. If we do, we run the risk of becoming blind to our foibles, and allowing others to suffer as a result.

# CHAPTER 6

## GETTING THE JOB DONE

### A BLUEPRINT FOR ACTION

Many board members feel somewhat confused about their roles as board members. This is quite understandable because no handbook exists describing the functional responsibilities of pension fund board members. So, let's acknowledge this condition of ignorance and look at the problem at a basic level. Pension fund boards are made up of people who have come together to serve a purpose: to pay pensions at the lowest cost to the contributors and the lowest risk of nonpayment to the plan participants. To assist board members in accomplishing that goal, we turn our attention to a checklist of sorts. This checklist gives board members a way to give order and meaning to the discharge of their individual and collective purpose. Put another way, the following might best be considered as a blueprint for action. Many details will have to be developed by each board to make the blueprint useful as a working document. Once the details specific to each pension fund are completed, the blueprint is transformed into a map and compass to guide the board. Here's the checklist:

- Develop a mission statement.
- Develop the data to write or update a strategic plan:
    Analyze size and timing of emerging liabilities.
    Analyze cost of funding and stability of contributions.
    Analyze funded ratio.
    Evaluate all actuarial assumptions.
    Assess risk: How much can the plan afford to lose and still
        meet all of its obligations?
- Construct or update the strategic plan:
    Calculate the hurdle rate of return.

Develop the cash plan and the length of the cash planning period.

Integrate asset allocation to meet current and future pension benefit payments.

* Implement the strategic plan:

Examine your present portfolio.

Compare present portfolio to cash plan.

Make appropriate rebalancing adjustments in the portfolio to accommodate the needs of the cash plan.

* Monitor and measure the progress in accomplishing strategic plan objectives:

Examine the magnitude and direction of change in the funded ratio.

Examine the magnitude and direction of change of the cost of funding.

Examine the magnitude and direction of change of the hurdle rate of return.

Examine how well our cash plan is matched up against emerging liabilities.

Based on the progress made (or lost), the board must go through the entire checklist periodically to make midcourse corrections. So the final item in the checklist is this: Repeat the above as often as necessary to continue to plan for the future and its obligations.

This checklist underscores the board member's true function. Some might argue that the board has more important things to do with its time than concentrate on the above issues: things such as manager performance or investment performance reviews, for example. Yet, what could be more important to a pension fund board than understanding *how* it is going to pay its pensions? Given appropriate attention to detail, the checklist becomes a map and compass for a pension fund. By means of the strategic plan, the board charts its course. And, while there are other tasks a board must typically handle, none is more important that those outlined above.

## STAFF AND BOARD

Many pension fund boards spend their time doing things that are more appropriately handled by the board's staff. The relationship between staff and board is made unnecessarily complicated when a board is not discharging its proper function. Just what should the relationship between the board and the staff be? First, we must remember that the board's job is to govern the fund and pay the pensions. To do this, it must delegate the important nuts and bolts tasks to others. This is where the executive staff comes in (vice president of pensions, executive director, etc.).

Delegation of authority from the board to the professional staff is required to accomplish the objectives of the plan. But this delegation does not relieve the board of its primary obligation to pay and prepare to pay all the pensions. Instead, the board requires others to carry out the details of board policy and directives. These others work under the direction of the executive staff.

One important role for the executive staff is to administrate and manage the operating side of the fund. This entails such tasks as budgeting, financial reporting, communications with plan participants, information systems, disbursements of pension checks, and so forth. For the most part, the responsibility for these operations is vested in the senior operating executive of the pension fund. This person reports to the board and is their right-hand man. He has full responsibility for making sure the plan is administered effectively and should have authority from the board to carry out these functions.

In matters of plan governance, the executive staff should be a valuable resource to the board and be an integral part of the fund's policymaking apparatus. This means that the senior staff will have an important role to play in developing, constructing, implementing, monitoring, and fine-tuning the pension fund's strategic plan. The executive staff should coordinate and supervise the entire process on behalf of the board. Moreover, the executive staff is responsible for communicating the mission of the pension fund to the rest of the plan's organization. This is important because it lends a sense of purpose to guide the organization in fulfillment of the fund's mission.

Finally, the board must remember that their staff is comprised of human beings. These people are not mere lackeys who exist only to do the board's bidding. They are professionals who deserve to be treated with respect and dignity. Above all, staff members deserve recognition for their work done on behalf of the plan and its participants. Board members would do well to remember to treat their staff as partners. In return, staff members will respond and redouble their efforts on behalf of the plan.

## DECISION MAKING

Decision making cannot be avoided. It has often been said that you have to break a few eggs to make an omelet. Pension funds are no exception to this adage. To guide the board in decision making, the following rules should be considered:

1. *Does it make sense?*
   While it may seem obvious that the test of common sense be first applied to any decision, all too often decisions are not judged in this fashion. Common sense is an indispensable tool that can be used to cut through ambiguity and nonsense. Use it often and better decision making will result.

2. *How does this decision benefit the plan participants? If it does not have a benefit to the plan participants, why is this decision under consideration?*
   Put in another way, board members must ask, "Why are we here, and how does this decision assist us in fulfilling our mission?" Often we get caught up in the activities of the moment and neglect our fundamental mission. Each and every minute of board time should be spent in the highest and best service of the plan participants. Other considerations must not be allowed to intrude or interfere with this primary objective.

3. *All decisions will not be right.*
   Mistakes are inevitable. Bad decisions are corrected by making new decisions, which hopefully are better, but may not be. So don't worry about being wrong; everybody is wrong from time to time. Successful folks don't view their failures or mistakes as failures. They view these errors as ways to get better and get the job done.

4. *You will never have all the facts, so don't think you will.*
   If we wait to gather *all* the facts prior to making a decision, we will have a long wait indeed. Facts must be gathered, interpreted, and communicated to others to make effective decisions. Yet the board must balance the need to collect enough facts to guide decision making with the need to make the decision in a timely way. We will never have enough facts on hand to render any decision 100 percent effective. Life is simply too complex. Once a commonsense-oriented course can be discerned, gathering more facts becomes counterproductive.

5. *Often, making the decision is the most important decision. Without a decision, no action can take place.*
   This is not to say that decisions cannot, or should not, be tabled or postponed from time to time. It is just that the business of the pension fund must be carried out. This requires that decisions be made in service of the fund's objectives.

6. *A decision not to act is still a decision.*
   This may seem obvious, but a decision not made has consequences that can be every bit as important as decisions actually taken. Therefore, deciding not to decide must be done with forethought and care given to the consequences of inaction.

7. *People, not computers, make decisions.*
   Computers have so permeated the pension fund world that we sometimes forget the importance of the human element in decision making. Computers are built, programmed, and manipulated to produce an output. And while this output may seem objective because a machine has been involved, most computer-derived data is intended to serve somebody's desire to persuade somebody else. Board members must be alert for the element of persuasive intent on the part of those who present computer-driven answers as correct. We must stand ready to challenge those whose conclusions do not meet the dual tests of common sense and congruence with the objectives of the pension fund.

8. *Humility is an art form.*
   When you think you are on a hot streak of brilliant decisions, you are most prone to error. Listen, be patient, evaluate with a clear head, be honest about the circumstances, and make the decision to benefit the plan participants.

## GAMESMANSHIP

All gamesmanship revolves around one simple principle: Yield to a man's tastes, and he will yield to your interests. This reminds me of a story told by a local school board member. The school board had decided to expand the auditorium to include an orchestra pit. The cost was $150,000 and, needless to say, there were dissenting voices about this price. When the board tallied up the votes, there was a split decision. Obviously, no orchestra pit would be built. This board member was particularly observant of the scene. He noted that one of his fellow board members, a dissenting vote, had a daughter in the band. This board member approached the dissenter and said, "Wouldn't it be nice if you could see your daughter play in the band at school functions?" The dissenter agreed and understood if there were no orchestra pit, it would be impossible to have the band play there. The dissenter then changed his vote, and the orchestra pit was built.

The interesting thing here is not that an orchestra pit was built or not built. It is simply that we should note that virtually everyone will play games from time to time to accomplish what they see as an appropriate objective. There is no way to avoid gamesmanship, so wishful thinking that games will disappear is inappropriate to the task at hand. Instead, we must ask ourselves not whether the games will be played, but rather *towards what end will the games be played?*

There is a simple rule for board members to follow with respect to gamesmanship. It is this: Does the outcome of the game help the board pay the pensions at the lowest cost to the contributors and the lowest risk of nonpayment of benefits to the plan participants? Should any board member engage in games that do not meet this test, then these games are irrelevant at best, and wantonly destructive at worst. If, on the other hand, the games meet the above rule, then "Play ball!"

## RELATIONSHIPS

Pension funds are no different from any other human endeavor. They involve people who know each other. Sometimes it is the business of the pension fund that brings people in relation to one another. Sometimes relationships pre-date involvement with a pension fund's business. There is nothing inherently nefarious about any human relationship. Indeed, this is the way the world works. If we know somebody, we are more likely to know what kind of a person he or she is through having had experience with them. Knowing who we think people are through having worked with them in the past makes us want either to work with them again or avoid working with them, depending on our prior experiences. This does not mean there is some kind of a worldwide conspiracy for people to want to do business with those with whom they have successfully done business in the past. It simply means that human beings are more comfortable with the people they know than they are with the people they do not know.

As with gamesmanship, relationships should be judged by a simple rule. If the end to be served in the relationship is in line with the objectives of the pension fund, then, absent mischief or wrongdoing, the relationship serves the pension fund well. This rule should apply to relationships that might exist or develop between or among managers, brokers, consultants, board members, staff members, actuaries, attorneys, and accountants. The point is not *that* there is a relationship, but rather *towards what end* is the relationship? Board members must ask themselves, "Has the *effect* of this relationship helped us or hurt us in our effort to pay all the pensions at the lowest cost to the contributors and the lowest risk of nonpayment of benefits to the plan participants?" If the relationship has neither hurt nor helped, then, absent wrongdoing, the relationship is irrelevant. If the relationship has hurt, it should be broken. If the relationship has helped, it should be encouraged.

## PEELING THE ONION

Rome wasn't built in a day. When it comes to effective board action on matters of policy and implementation, peeling the onion is an apt description of problem resolution. This is a way to describe the whole process because you cannot get people to change established ways of doing things overnight. To get the job done, you have to take things one step at a time and listen carefully to all those involved. Things have a natural order and progress at a speed that can be difficult, if not impossible, to change. Understand this, expect it, work within the real world's constraints and you will be more effective in the long run. A Russian proverb says, the slower you go, the farther you get. There is great wisdom in this. Be aware that things take time. Here is a suggested order for peeling an onion without too many tears:

- Stop, look, listen.
- Assess the situation.
- Communicate your assessment to others and listen to what they have to say.
- Digest and think about what has been learned.
- Prioritize the issues at hand and the issues ahead.
- Decide what is doable as a next step, and what must be reserved for doing at a later date.

- Communicate to others and listen to what they have to say.
- Formulate an approach to the problem.
- Communicate your approach to others and listen to what they have to say.
- Ask others to support you in the effort.
- Pursue a decision.
- Implement the decision.
- Monitor the results.
- Repeat as necessary to peel down the next layer of the onion.

While this process can be continued indefinitely, the order of magnitude of the problems to be solved should diminish over time. The larger issues will take a lot of time to resolve and will consist of many, many subproblems. Each of the larger issues must be attacked and resolved in a careful, relentless, and deliberate manner, tackling layer by layer as circumstances allow. To the greatest degree possible, smaller issues should be made subordinate in importance to the larger issues. Progress on all issues will require peeling the onion of habit and existing practice. The end of this effort is clear: we want to be able to pay all the pensions at the lowest cost to the contributors and the lowest risk of nonpayment of benefits to the plan participants.

## BOARD LEADERSHIP

There's no getting around this issue. Groups of people require leadership to operate effectively, and pension boards are no exception. Let's describe what leadership is not, to better understand what it is. Here is an illustration from an old TV series called "Battlestar Galactica." The villains in the series were robots known as Cylons. The prime mission of these robots was to destroy human beings. In one episode, three Cylons in their fighter spacecraft engaged the humans in combat. During the engagement, the Cylon craft was hit and damaged. To deal with this life-threatening situation, the three Cylons talked endlessly about what to do. While talking about what to do, they crashed. The moral is simple: Consensus-based decision making is a flawed strategy.

So what is the right strategy? As board members, leadership is required of all of us at one time or another. But generally, groups of people will only consent to being led by those who have the respect of the group. What's more, that leadership requires the continued support of those folks who have agreed to be led. This is where *individual* leadership is required from each board member to keep the leader in line and to test his mettle. The leader must lead no faster than the consensus of the group will allow, but he must lead nonetheless. It is a fine art, and indispensable to effective board action.

## SIMPLE SELL DISCIPLINE

As we have discussed, pension funds are perceived to be holding assets in virtual perpetuity. This misguided notion begs the real issues of what pension assets are being accumulated for. As we have seen, incorporation of an effective sell discipline provides a way to harvest gains in long-term assets in service of the pension fund's financial objective. We have already looked at rules to govern the sales process from the standpoint of the pension fund's liabilities. But here we will set forth a simple way to get the job done with respect to the capital markets, using market and statistical road signs as a guide. The reality of the capital markets is that there are always assets that are overvalued and those that are undervalued. Sell disciplines don't have to be complicated to be effective. You don't have to have a big computer with a complex program to tell you when to sell.

Instead of a complex system, we begin by examining the historic road signs with respect to each type of long-term asset we hold. We use the readily available data to determine which assets should be harvested, and where new assets should be sown. Each asset class will have its own set of road signs, and these data will not necessarily overlap those signs for other asset classes.

Illustrated in Figure 6-1 is a simplified illustration of how to implement a sell discipline to pay pensions, and a simple buy discipline to help find value for long-term asset growth. This hypothetical illustration involves having assessed the value of the large capitalization domestic stock market to relevant historic road signs, and having assessed the small capitalization domestic stocks to their relevant historic road signs. In this illustration, the large capitalization stocks were found to be overvalued, and profit was taken from them by selling off a part of the portfolio. Proceeds from the sale are then earmarked for the cash-matched bond portfolio. The small cap stocks, on the other hand, were seen to be undervalued, and therefore, contributions and dividends are applied to purchases

**FIGURE 6–1**

**Application of Simplistic Sell Discipline and Buy Discipline Based on Values in Market Relative to Road Signs Appropriate to Each Asset Class**

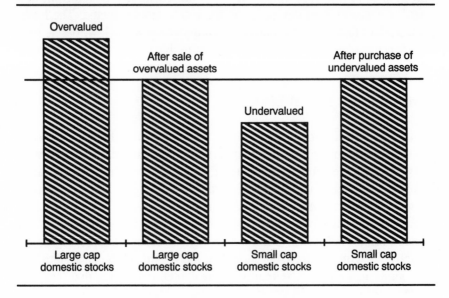

of these securities. Naturally, in the real world, these decisions are more complicated. Even so, it is a good idea to set up a method similar to that shown to assist in the purchase and sale of assets into and out of the long-term portfolio.

One more time, it should be noted: This is *not* to be confused with market timing aimed at maximization of gains in a timed portfolio. Instead, it is taking advantage of the natural ebb and flow of value in the capital markets to harvest gains in service of paying pensions and to place investment dollars into assets that appear undervalued.

## ACTIVE-MANAGER ASSESSMENT AND SELECTION

While a passive strategy with an integral sell discipline is far superior to most active management of long-term assets, it is possible for certain discrete active managers to outperform the averages. And, since most pension funds do hire active managers, we would do well to consider the assessment and selection of those managers with great care. In all these discussions, we must remember that conventional methods of investment performance measurements are made *gross* of management fees. Since management fees vary greatly among managers, this measurement method distorts comparisons of investment performance among managers as well as to the applicable indexes. In our active management program, then, we must make sure that the active manager can outperform the applicable index plus the management fees required to purchase that performance.

Most, if not all, consultants assess and select asset managers on a subjective and current performance basis without regard for consistency over the longer term. The consultants rarely identify the process under which candidates are evaluated and recommended. The issue of concern for the consultant is how to select a manager who will have the highest comfort level with the plan sponsor subject to current relative performance. Instead of this methodology, consider an alternative process for manager assessment and selection.

This process was developed by Richard C. Harris, who assisted in the compilation of this book after some 15 years as a public pension fund board member. The essence of the process is to develop a simple matrix, with the names of managers down the left-hand side of the page, and each year of the most recent 10 years at the top of the page. Reading across the page, for each manager, is the performance number achieved by each manager during each year of the 10 years shown. The matrix uses 10-year rolling periods, so as each year ends, the earliest year is dropped off, and the newest year is added to the matrix.

This process allows the board to see all the managers' 10- year performance numbers against themselves, against the hurdle rate of return, against inflation, against the appropriate index, and against other managers. The process is especially important in flat or down markets where board members can see how well managers are able to retain the gains they have earned during the good years. This ensures that board members won't get caught up in a hot-manager syndrome where the hottest manager of a given period is hired and retained indiscriminately. The process also prevents excessive manager and portfolio turnover, both of which are exceedingly costly. The following specific factors must be examined when selecting a prospective manager:

1. Review and comparison against existing manager base.
2. Ten-year review of performance against indexes, hurdle rates, inflation, and peers.

3. Strict examination of the prospective manager's performance in flat and down markets.
4. Understandable sell discipline.
5. Manager style and returns evaluated on a volatility-adjusted basis.
6. History of organization and continuity of key personnel.
7. Normal due diligence.

Table 6-1 shows an example of the Harris matrix as applied to an actual group of equity managers.

The Harris matrix is useful for the ongoing process of investment manager performance as well as for the selection of new managers. Regardless of how it is used, though, it is important that all managers be examined on the same basis. This is not always an easy task, as some managers will attempt to present their performance data in a more favorable light than it might otherwise deserve. Some of the distortions employed by prospective managers involve the disclosure of only that performance data that demonstrates a superior record, while omitting data that might be less impressive. Towards this end, managers might select only those numbers relating to a particularly well-performing account similar in some way to the prospective client's account. If the prospect is a public fund, maybe only public fund data will be shown. If the prospect is small, maybe only small account data will be shown. There are obviously endless variations on this theme, where managers select some group of high-performing assets and present it as representative of their overall performance as active managers.

To defeat these sleights of hand, we must insist that all of a manager's accounts be included in any presentation of prior performance. What's more, all numbers must be shown *net* of management fees. Even though showing net performance is unconventional, the board must *insist* on it to be able to compare one manager against another, and against both the index and the needs of our pension fund. Only by subtracting fees can we determine whether a manager has earned his keep. Otherwise, we have no idea what we are paying for.

Another very important item to keep in mind when going through the process of manager selection is to make sure that the personnel responsible for having posted the track record under examination are still with the firm and will be devoting their time to your account. Check *who* was responsible for past performance, and make sure you are getting the right bill of goods.

Active management is probably not the best way to have long-term pension fund assets invested. It is too expensive for the investment perfor-

**TABLE 6–1**
**The Harris Matrix**

Equity Manager Composite Returns
(% Annual Periods—Quartile Rank)

| Manager | 1979 - Q | 1980 - Q | 1981 - Q | 1982 - Q | 1983 - Q | 1984 - Q | 1985 - Q | 1986 - Q | 1987 - Q | Total | 9 Yr. Av. | 1988 |
|---|---|---|---|---|---|---|---|---|---|---|---|---|
| A | 23.5 - 2 | 39.3 - 1 | 3.1 - 2 | 33.9 - 1 | 33.3 - 1 | 1.3 - 4 | 40.5 - 1 | 27.3 - 1 | 9.9 - 1 | 212.1 | 23.57 | 10.1 |
| B | 36.4 - 1 | 26.6 | 8.5 - 1 | 33.3 - 1 | 32.2 - 1 | 13.8 - 1 | 37.2 - 1 | 16.0 - 3 | 2.2 - 4 | 206.2 | 22.91 | 21.0 |
| C | 25.9 - 1 | 45.3 - 1 | 5.5 - 1 | 25.2 - 3 | 29.8 - 1 | 11.2 - 1 | 44.2 - 1 | 13.3 - 4 | 1.6 - 4 | 202.4 | 22.45 | 24.9 |
| D | 19.8 - 3 | 42.2 - 1 | 3.0 - 2 | 28.5 - 2 | 41.3 - 1 | 4.0 - 2 | 25.0 - 4 | 11.5 - 4 | 14.8 - 1 | 190.1 | 21.13 | 24.1 |
| E | 21.4 | 54.4 | (4.8) | 32.5 | 21.1 | 0.4 | 29.8 | 17.4 | 12.8 | 185.0 | 20.56 | 10.2 |
| F | 20.0 | 53.8 | (2.7) | 28.7 | 40.2 | (8.8) | 27.7 | 9.0 | 13.6 | 181.5 | 20.16 | 6.4 |
| G | 24.0 - 2 | 30.7 - 2 | 5.3 - 1 | 28.0 - 1 | 25.1 - 1 | 6.3 - 2 | 33.1 - 1 | 23.6 - 1 | (0.7) - 4 | 180.2 | 20.02 | 18.4 |
| H | 20.9 - 3 | 27.0 - 3 | 7.4 - 1 | 29.9 - 1 | 24.5 - 1 | 9.2 - 1 | 31.1 - 2 | 18.4 - 2 | 3.0 - 3 | 171.4 | 19.04 | 13.7 |
| I | 28.2 - 1 | 22.0 - 4 | 8.9 - 1 | 23.0 - 3 | 26.7 - 1 | 9.0 - 1 | 31.0 - 2 | 23.1 - 1 | (0.7) - 4 | 171.2 | 19.02 | 22.4 |
| J | 19.8 - 3 | 38.9 - 1 | 0.9 - 2 | 26.6 - 1 | 26.6 - 1 | 7.4 - 1 | 27.6 - 3 | 15.3 - 3 | (3.6) - 4 | 159.5 | 17.72 | 20.2 |
| K | 17.6 - 4 | 30.0 - 3 | (2.3) - 3 | 11.1 - 4 | 18.4 - 2 | 6.9 - 2 | 33.1 - 1 | 21.1 - 1 | 4.9 - 2 | 140.8 | 15.64 | 12.5 |
| L | NA | NA | NA | 28.1 | 21.4 | (3.4) | 38.2 | 23.5 | 0.4 | NA | NA | 20.9 |
| M | 18.7 | 29.0 | 25.9 | 41.5 | 37.2 | 17.3 | 36.0 | 19.0 | 10.4 | 261.1 | 29.00 | 29.1 |
| S&P 500 | 18.6 | 32.5 | (4.9) | 21.6 | 22.5 | 6.2 | 31.6 | 18.6 | 5.27 | 151.97 | 16.8 | 16.5 |

mance being delivered. Regardless of how we look at active-manager selection, however, two factors are *always* working against the active manager: management fees and execution costs. We have looked briefly at the issue of management fees; now we turn our attention to execution costs to see how these must be managed to get the job done. Execution costs are significant and have been estimated to subtract a full percentage point from the average equity manager's investment performance record. Consequently, if we are to have any active management at all, we should consider this issue very carefully.

## EXECUTION MANAGEMENT

Most money managers delegate the trading process. As with any area of expertise, some people are good at it, and some people aren't. Trading is no exception. Therefore, it is incumbent on pension fund trustees and professionals alike not to assume that just because some people can manage money, they automatically know how to manage executions. And execution costs, however small, add up to big dollars in the aggregate.

In this day and age of the billion dollar deal and the $20,000 family sedan, pennies just don't get much respect. Gone are the days of penny candy. Instead, pennies are often regarded as a nuisance. They collect in our pockets as dead weight, and we are forever trying to get rid of them. The toll booths on the Pennsylvania Turnpike have hand-lettered signs that read, ''NO PENNIES.'' Nobody picks up a penny should it be seen on a sidewalk in the city. Restaurants have little penny cups to collect pennies for use by patrons who need them for change. These circumstances have conditioned us to think of the lowly penny as not really having much value. But pennies do have value if we add enough of them together. And that is exactly the point when it comes to the scrutiny of pension fund transaction costs.

The easiest illustration of the importance of trading costs is available in the equity markets. Let's assume that a $10 billion pension fund has 40 percent of its assets in equities with an average share price of $40. Let's further assume that the portfolio turns over one and a half times a year in transactions that aggregate 150 million shares. In this illustration, at 7 cents a share, the annual transaction cost is $10.5 million. How many pennies are there in $10.5 million? Our little postal scale shows that there are about 10 pennies to the ounce. At this rate, there would be 3,281 *tons* of pennies in $10.5 million. And, if we saved but one penny per share in trading costs, the savings would total $1.5 million. That's a lot of pennies.

## REDUCTION OF TRADING COSTS

An example of one relatively minor way we can manage our trading costs is to reduce our number of trades. Why? Because, if other factors are held constant, managers with high portfolio turnover will generate incremental expenses to the pension fund in the form of additional custodial fees. These fees are small, but they do add up. Portfolio turnover is difficult for trustees to control after a manager has been hired. And, as it impairs a manager's latitude of action, it is probably not desirable to pursue after the fact. Nevertheless, if trustees are interviewing two managers with similar performance records, the manager with lower turnover is likely to provide the most cost-effective management over the longer term.

The most significant way we can control our execution costs is to work closely with our managers and brokers to enhance our understanding and control of problem areas. There are significant hidden costs in trading securities, such as in settlements and markups. Let's look at how we can do better in our management of this area.

## A FEW BASICS ABOUT EXECUTION MANAGEMENT

In the context of this discussion, it might be helpful to expose some of the lesser-known elements of execution management. To begin, we must first look at how the money management, brokerage, and pension fund industry interact with each other.

In the typical money management firm are those who establish investment policy and strategy, those who select securities for purchase and sale, those who market and sell the firm's services to clients, and those who are charged with the actual buying and selling of the selected securities. The people who buy and sell are known as the money manager's traders. These traders work with any number of other firms known as broker-dealers (sometimes referred to as brokerage firms or, simply, brokers). Some broker-dealers are small and some are large. Regardless of size, however, broker-dealers are selected by the money manager on a trade-by-trade basis. That is, a broker-dealer is selected to execute a trade on behalf of the money manager and his client every time a trade is made. This selection can be based on a wide variety of reasons, ranging from precedent and friendship, all the way to selection based on some specialized area of broker expertise in a given trading area. Importantly, the pension fund does not govern the selection of brokers or the trading process. The pension fund can only establish ground rules within which the managers must operate.

Broadly speaking, there are two types of trades: agency trades and principal trades. An agency trade is one in which the broker is the *agent* of the money manager (and indirectly, of the pension fund that has hired the money manager). In an agency trade, the broker charges a commission on the trade and never takes title to the securities. It is important to recognize that in an agency trade all the brokerage costs are disclosed to the money manager and his clients. A principal trade is a very different beast. Sometimes known as a net trade, a principal trade is one in which the broker sells a security that *he* owns to the money manager. In the parlance of the industry, a principal trade does not involve a broker at all. Instead, the broker in a principal trade is referred to as a dealer of securities, giving rise to the name broker-dealer. The dealer makes his money by selling securities out of his inventory at a markup to his cost. It does not matter whether the dealer acquired the securities moments before reselling them or months beforehand. What matters to the dealer is that he gets the highest markup possible on each sale. The key thing to remember here is that the costs of a principal trade are hidden from everyone but the dealer. He never has to disclose his costs; he simply quotes the sales price and we take it or leave it.

Finally, we should look briefly at the whole issue of soft dollars. *Soft dollars* is an investment industry term used to describe a brokerage practice of setting aside a certain amount of commission dollars for use by a pension fund in purchasing goods or services. If the broker charges, say, 7 cents per share as a commission, perhaps two pennies of the commission is diverted into a special soft-dollar account designated for the use of the pension fund client. The broker gets the balance of the commission to operate his business. The pension fund now submits approved invoices to the broker for payment from the soft-dollar account. These invoices may cover the purchase of computers, software, research, consulting services, publications, or even office furniture, to name a few commonly purchased items. The only criterion for use of soft dollars is that the purchases benefit the plan participants.

Why are soft dollars used instead of simply getting a direct reduction in commissions? The answer to this question is rooted in the way pension fund administration is viewed by many, particularly in the public sector. The boldface truth is that pension fund administration is often seen as a low priority issue. Because of this perception, the administrative budgets of many pension funds are squeezed to the point where essential purchases become all but impossible. Soft dollars are a way to handle this reality and enable the pension fund to operate more effectively than its administrative budget might otherwise allow.

Alternatively, some money managers also set up soft-dollar programs for their use in the purchase of services, particularly research services. This is a way for the manager to stretch his management fees and improve his bottom line.

With these few thoughts in mind, let's turn our attention back to execution management. Towards that end, here are a few rules for dealing with the important, but often overlooked area, of execution management:

## FOUR SIMPLE RULES FOR BETTER EXECUTIONS

### *Rule No. 1: Don't Let Amateurs Manage Our Trades*

Broker-bashing is fast replacing Monday-morning-quarterbacking as the fastest growing national pastime. To date, all studies regarding agency commissions assume that the broker executing an agency trade is to be held responsible for the entire process. The reasoning goes that it is the broker and the broker alone who controls the commission rate, manages the soft dollars, and governs the market impact of the trades. These studies assume that each order is given to the broker at the opening of the trading day, and that the individual broker has the discretionary power to determine the time and price of the execution. While this approach works well on paper, trades seldom happen this smoothly in the real world.

Trustees must remember that their manager is hired for his ability to manage assets, and not for his ability to trade. By experience and training, many managers have not been exposed to this aspect of the business. Sometimes, managers do not realize the number of dollars that slip through the cracks through inexperienced or inept trading.

Once, when a manager was hired to manage a substantial sum of pension assets, the first trade consisted of the following instructions from the manager's trader: "Buy me a couple of hundred thousand zero coupon bonds." After giving his order in this way, the trader promptly hung up. Fortunately, the broker knew immediately there was a problem and called the manager to determine the exact dollar amount the manager wished to spend, the face amount of the purchase, the desired interest rate, and the time period for executing the order.

When the pension fund was advised of this occurrence, the chief investment officer called the manager to inquire about the background of the trader. In response, the manager characterized the trader as a hard-working, honest individual whose previous employment had been as the manager of a health club owned by the manager and his partners.

On a second occasion, another manager placed a limit order for 500,000 shares of a stock listed on the New York Stock Exchange. The broker asked the manager if the shares were "held." That is to say, may the broker exercise discretion to effect a lower price if he was able to do so? The manager's reply was "We don't quite understand how you do these things, but of course you can." This manager had over 20 years' experience and at this date manages assets in excess of $8 billion.

The moral of the story is readily apparent. Many times, our brokers are given orders that make little sense in the trading world. Recognize that good performance on the part of our managers does not necessarily make them capable or knowledgeable as traders, as there is wide variation in the abilities of money managers in this regard. Finally, both we and our managers should be made aware that the trading desk function represents a cost that directly affects the manager's bottom line as well as ours.

### Rule No. 2: Hold Our Broker Accountable, but Only for What Is Under His Control

The costs associated with equity transactions have been the subject of most pension fund scrutiny. The first criterion for evaluating the broker is the true net cost to the pension fund. This is simply defined as the specified commission rate minus any soft-dollar rebate received by the pension fund for its direct use. Soft dollars that inure to the manager's benefit and only indirectly to that of the fund are not counted in this evaluation. Using this simple formula, all costs are in real dollars, and the accountability of all parties is known.

Since, as trustees, we are never in a position to know who is truly accountable for the market impact, it is hard to bash brokers for something that is not under their control. Of course, trustees can arbitrarily set commission rates but must recognize that cheaper commissions alone do not result in better overall execution.

Instead, each manager should be closely monitored, along with his or her corresponding brokerage charges. Then, the pension fund and its managers should work cooperatively to identify problems and lower overall transaction costs.

### Rule No. 3: Beware of Brokers Bearing Net Trades

A fertile area for us to consider is the issue of buying listed and unlisted stocks traded over the counter on a net basis or for no commission whatsoever. Recent studies have shown that net transactions have grown tremendously as a percentage of total equity transactions. Typically, brokers prefer net transactions since they need not disclose their true markup. Let's look at this practice and see if there really is such a thing as a free lunch.

The national average for agency commissions is approximately 6 to 7 cents per share or lower, depending on size of trade and volume. We saw one manager who placed an order to purchase 200,000 shares of stock listed on the National Association of Securities Dealers Automated Quotation (NASDAQ) at 22 bid and 22½ offered.

The first broker who was given the order offered to do the trade at 22½ net or without a commission. The next three brokers executing part of the same order offered the same price that was readily accepted by the manager's trader. (In this case, the manager's trader was his ex-personal secretary!) The final portion of the order was placed with a broker who does not do any equity trades on a net basis. This broker purchased the shares at 22 and charged his customary 5 cents per share commission.

Because she did not understand execution practices, the manager's trader complained to the agency broker that because he charged a commission, he wasn't competitive with the other brokers. In reality, the three net traders were charging the manager 10 times the commission charged by the agency trader. How were they doing this? Simple. Two of the net traders went into the market, purchased the shares at 22, and then resold them to the manager at 22½. The other net trader had the shares in his inventory and sold them to the manager at 22½, on a cost of 21⅞ Neat trick, isn't it?

But think about it. If each of the traders handled 50,000 shares, then the net traders had charged at least $67,500 in hidden trading costs to the pension fund. While in this example nothing unscrupulous is at hand, the true costs of the trades remained hidden from both the manager and the pension fund customer.

At other times, we have watched market-makers deliberately move the price of the stock to be purchased up one eighth or even one fourth of a point. This practice is more commonly known as frontrunning. It's illegal but it does happen. We have seen actual commission charges of 75 cents or more per share. It is no coincidence that the Street likes doing net trades with unsuspecting or unknowledgeable managers. While not all net trades are a problem, probably the only defense against the unscrupulous net traders is to insist that *all* equity transactions be done on an agency basis where the true costs are readily apparent.

Some market-makers argue that the markups taken on net trades are merely fair compensation for maintaining market liquidity. They complain that mere commissions don't take into account the cost of holding inventories of securities for sale and purchase. Nevertheless, while these are legitimate concerns, it does not follow that a pension fund or any other fiduciary should bear these costs indiscriminately and without disclosure.

To round out this discussion, let's look at fixed-income trading, where few trades are done on an agency basis. While about 60 percent of most public pension fund assets are in fixed-income securities, the costs of trading these investments have been completely overlooked in almost all the studies. This seems especially ironic when it is possible that the costs of trading bonds may represent the bulk of most pension fund overall trading costs.

Fixed-income trades have almost always been done on a principal basis. Dealers buy fixed-income securities and resell them at a profit. Instead of charging a commission, they charge a markup.

Instead of us having an agent executing trades on our behalf, we have a dealer executing trades on his own behalf.

As in the case of NASDAQ stocks, the issues of inventory costs and market liquidity are real. Fixed-income dealers are faced with many problems in these areas. Certain types of government-backed bonds are illiquid, sometimes for the short term, and sometimes permanently. Some fixed-income securities are fraught with difficulties related to settlement and delivery. Accordingly, it is simply unfair to insist that fixed-income dealers bear the entire brunt of these difficulties. Clearly, there should be additional compensation for difficult services honestly rendered.

What constitutes a fair market on each type of investment should be subject to honest and open discussion between buyer and broker. We should work only with those brokers willing to discuss their execution problems and costs in an open fashion well in advance of executing fixed-income trades on our behalf. This practice will allow the parties to come to a mutual agreement upon fair markups. Agreeing on these preapproved levels of markup will allow the broker to search the market looking for the best transaction while acting as *our* agent and not as *his* own agent.

An interesting side benefit to the pure agency approach is that the commission expended on this type of transaction becomes readily available for soft-dollar consideration. This option is not an alternative when the net traders are allowed to run freely through our equity and fixed-income portfolios without oversight.

### *Rule No. 4: Our Portfolio Is Our Portfolio*

This rule applies equally to equity and to fixed-income execution management. Put simply, there is much to be gained and nothing to be lost by focusing on the cost and effectiveness of the execution of our trades. So it is up to us to take control of the process. Do not let the fox watch over our hen house.

Make sure our managers understand that execution management is important to us. Make sure we are comfortable with the execution management we are being provided. Seek out and instruct our managers to use those brokers who trade only on an agency basis.

The assets entrusted to our care are important enough to warrant our attention throughout the management process, not just when we examine a manager's performance. Remember, many, but not all, managers and their traders are ignorant of execution management. This lack of knowledge costs them dearly in terms of lower performance. What's more, poorly managed execution costs our pension plan many hard dollars.

### *Plan of Action for More Effective Execution Management*

1. Find a tough, honest, and hard-nosed broker who will work for us and with whom we can discuss our current brokerage and execution problems. Treat him as we would a prized advisor. Let him give us insight into our actual cost structure and identify those areas where a change of policy at the board level will be effective.

2. Establish a control desk to ensure continuous monitoring of all our managers and serve as a benchmark for our brokers. Some problems will become readily apparent, and corrective measures can be instituted immediately rather than waiting for a formal study to be finished.

3. Recognize the value and limitations of the current cost studies concerning brokerage commissions.

4. Train our internal staff to be sensitive to the problems and costs of brokerage execution. This type of training is available at no cost through some of the specialized cost-control brokers.

5. Seek out our true costs and evaluate all our brokers in terms of dollars for which they can be held accountable.

6. Insist on full disclosure of all commissions or markups whether done on an agency or dealer basis.

7. Recognize that different categories of investments have different trading-cost structures associated with them. Be willing to pay a fair price for services rendered.

# CHAPTER 7

## RESPONSIBLE STEWARDSHIP

In this final chapter, we will examine some of the more complex philosophical and behavioral quirks involved in pension fund governance. Stewardship is not an easy task. Neither is it a job whose duties have been well delineated. Yet, we must be on constant guard to render the most effective and responsible governance possible. Towards this end, the following thoughts and essays are intended to provoke thought and give rise to better and more effective action.

### THE PRUDENT-MAN RULE, MINDLESS ACTION, AND THE URGE TO AGREE

There is silent danger in the prudent-man rule, that comes, in part, from man's inclination to find safety in numbers. When our neighbors and peers are all doing something, we have a tendency to label the activity as acceptable. In pension fund management, the prudent-man rule is made an integral part of the board member's role. But the prudent-man rule assumes that what other prudent men are doing is, in fact, prudent. This interpretation separates the judgment of an action as prudent from the consequences of that action being imprudent. Instead, board members are asked merely to look around them to see what other prudent men are doing as a guide for action. By this standard, when everybody else is doing something, it becomes OK for us to do it as well. But board members should be wary of applying the prudent-man rule indiscriminately. The late Bennett Goodspeed tells an interesting story that illustrates this danger as follows:

A 12-year-old was once invited to try his luck at a trout pond that was famous in its Michigan county. One hundred yards long, twenty yards wide, and three feet deep, this pond was loaded with rainbow and brown trout that ranged in size up to eight pounds. Its owner, a friend of the boy's father, smugly challenged the lad to catch as many as he could, knowing that the fish were amply fed pellet food and that even the most skilled trout fishermen had come up empty trying to tempt these prize trophies.

Thinking he was given a sneak preview of heaven, the boy ran down to the pond to pull in the spoils. Six hours later, he understood the reason for the owner's smugness. He tried flies, spinners, flat fish, minnows, worms, and even live frogs—all to no avail. Acting out of frustration, he threw most of his worms into the pond and sat on the bank watching their snaking motions on the pond's floor.

For 10 minutes, the trout watched warily. Then one small fish ate one of the worms. Ten minutes later, another small trout gulped down a slightly larger worm. Finally, after another five minutes, a big trout took a worm. The fish, feeling safe with the endorsement of one of the biggies, within seconds transformed the pond into churning white water, as it was every trout for himself. With a worm on the boy's hook, it was a slaughter, as the trout now operated with the illusion of safety. The boy soon stood proudly in front of the owner's door with a string of 15 three-five pounders. Somehow his father's friendship with this man was never quite the same.[1]

There are two points here. The prudent-man rule is not a perfect guide to rendering judgment. Men are vulnerable and prone to error when they watch how their contemporaries behave without doing their own critical examination. The "group-think" must not be a substitute for our own thinking.

The second point is perhaps more subtle. The fish in our story were safe as long as they ate pellet food. Once tempted by the worms, though, they became more easily preyed upon. Pellet food was boring, ordinary, and safe. The fish were used to an abundant, if unchanging, supply of pellets. In contrast, the worms appeared much more attractive. Pension fund board members must not be afraid to be boring, ordinary, and safe. More exciting alternatives to a responsible, careful, and deliberate approach do not speak to the need to pay pensions. We can get good and fat on pellets.

---

[1]Bennett Goodspeed, *The Tao Jones Average* (New York: E. P. Dutton, 1983).

A board member is charged to think, exercise judgment, and be on guard against illusions of safety. It can be folly to rush into every new and exciting investment opportunity due to boredom with the safe, secure way of doing things. The prudent-man rule is of no value unless, as pension fund board members, we understand that if we are all thinking alike maybe no one is thinking at all.

This all too human tendency to rely on others for assessments of a proper course of action can take many forms. One variation on the prudent-man rule problem stems from the embarrassment we feel when we don't understand something that everyone else seems to understand.

As the professional investment community develops ever more complex and confusing approaches to investing, a board member's willingness to say, "No, I don't understand," can be a powerful tool to be used to the benefit of the pension fund. "No" can be positive, especially when it is coupled with the statement, "I don't understand." The combination of two seemingly negative expressions can be a powerful and effective stewardship tool when used to clarify understanding before taking action.

Board members are faced with a continuing stream of investment concepts—many of which may be unfamiliar. The challenge of good stewardship is to understand these concepts, decide which are valid, and discard those that are not. In order to accomplish this stewardship process, the power of the phrase, "No, I don't understand," must be brought to bear on issues under examination. The reason for doing so is simple.

We live in a society replete with professions, and each one has developed its own obscure lexicon. As man acquired specialized knowledge, he learned to distinguish himself as a special person by creating word barriers between himself and his fellow man. As each vocation evolved its own vocabulary, words became barriers reinforcing the exclusivity of various professions. Today, we have legal professionals, medical professionals, investment professionals, among a wide variety of specialized pursuits. Each protects and perpetuates its self-interest through an intangible mask of words. The lay person is constantly required to break through these language barriers in order to find meaning and understanding. The most potent tool for this undertaking is the statement "No, I don't understand." Pension fund board members can use this simple statement to chisel through professional barriers.

If we can't communicate on equal terms, we can't arrive at understanding without which sound judgment is all but impossible. Remember, a cardinal rule of stewardship is to go no farther than our understanding.

In the mid-1980s, board members were told they needed to practice dynamic asset allocation, and portfolio insurance was represented as the key to that process. To support this thesis, the practitioners and purveyors of portfolio insurance supplied prospective clients with complex computer-driven concepts, described by new terms such as *floor levels of minimum return* and the *insurance premiums needed to maintain protection*. Even the phrase "dynamic asset allocation" itself was unclear. In all this talk, the most critical issue was left unattended. How do board members use portfolio insurance to achieve a pension fund's financial objective of paying pensions? As we'd expect, this was never made clear.

At the height of the popularity of portfolio insurance, I went to hear a presentation on the subject sponsored by a well-known consultant. The meeting was attended by a variety of the necessary experts. These professionals covered all phases of the subject. At the conclusion of the presentations, the sponsoring consultant opened the meeting to questions. This is where it got interesting (and poignant). For about 90 seconds, the room full of plan sponsors was engulfed in silence. No one, it seemed, wanted to open his mouth. I am certain many wanted to explore the subject, but nobody wanted to appear stupid. Finally, one lonely hand was raised. The consultant acknowledged it and this plan sponsor asked a direct question: "How do I *evaluate* portfolio insurance?" Again, there was an extended period of silence.

The silence ended when the first of the practitioners replied, "I don't know." The other practitioners followed suit. At this juncture, the consultant was asked the same question. He responded that the plan sponsor must try out portfolio insurance and see if his fund could develop a level of comfort and understanding about the value of the new concept. Not surprisingly, nobody asked any other questions, and the meeting broke at this point. As we walked out, I knew that portfolio insurance had made few converts that day. The moral of the story is this: If we do not understand something, and the concept cannot be explained to our satisfaction, then it will be impossible for us to act responsibly in our role as a steward of other peoples' assets.

And it is this same bad judgment that usually results in a loss of principal. Therefore, what obscures or defies understanding should be avoided. Never be embarrassed to actually say, *"No, I don't understand,"* right out loud. Remember, while silence is sometimes mistaken for understanding and agreement, if we don't understand, it is impossible to agree or disagree.

Despite our desire to do the right thing and be mindful of our purpose when we participate in board actions, we can end up doing things by rote, without giving the proper thought and attention to the matters at hand. Consider both sides of the following list:

*SHOPPING LIST*

| | |
|---|---|
| 5 lbs. flour | 5 percent cash equivalents |
| 5 lbs. sugar | 45 percent common stocks |
| 4 lbs. lean hamburger | 35 percent fixed income |
| 2 bunches celery | 10 percent mortgage participations |
| 2 bunches leeks | 5 percent real estate |

Lists are handy ways to organize our shopping and our work. I have a friend who begins each workday by filling out a sheet titled "Things I Gotta Do." Some people add another dimension to list-making: prioritizing into A lists, B lists, and C lists. But what makes for shopping sense does not automatically improve the investment process. Let's see why.

Perfunctory use of lists, or guidelines, brings with it a mindset of filling in the blanks. If I make the purchase, or fill the category, I have accomplished the required task. This is static activity, because completing the task does not fulfill an investment purpose. Effective investment policy is derived from an understanding that capital markets expand and contract according to underlying conditions that no list or prior set of guidelines can adequately anticipate. Investment policy must be dynamic. One important aspect of stewardship is to work continually to maintain the dynamism of investment policy. Without this continuous attention, we quickly lapse into the comfortable and mindless activity of filling in the blanks. This is to be guarded against as stewardship requires continual adaptation.

In the process of making lists, we must also guard against allowing the "gotta do" to overshadow the more important objective of managing a portfolio to pay pensions. We have all seen those asset allocation recommendations published in newsletters, which show a pie chart with "optimal asset allocation percentages." These charts purport to tell investors what the ideal shopping list looks like in the capital markets. But a pie chart can mislead a pension fund investor with its generalized instructions that have nothing to do with the pension fund's true needs. For example, let's say that the pie chart shows that a pension fund should have 2 percent of its portfolio in cash equivalents. What is the pension fund supposed to do if calculations show that 7 percent of its portfolio should be in cash equivalents to cover near-term pension benefit payments?

Let's take another look at the problem board members have with making asset allocation lists in a vacuum. This time, let's consider speed limits. Almost all open highway speed limits are set at 55 or 65 miles per hour. Does this mean that we must always drive at the posted speed limit? Obviously not. Sometimes weather conditions won't permit it. From time to time there is fog, road conditions are icy, or traffic is dangerously congested. To ignore these conditions would be foolish.

In a similar fashion, assume we were to have set investment guidelines that target an ideal allocation to real estate of 10 percent over time. Even with this ideal allocation in mind, if the real estate markets are overbuilt or overvalued, we cannot ignore the reality of the marketplace while our pension fund continues to try to fill in its ideal allocation of 10 percent. Instead, realize that an allocation is just a number—a number whose amount and speed of filling is subject to change, depending on the needs of the fund and on market conditions.

Stewardship is the key to a dynamic investment policy. Stewardship reflects the wisdom that markets expand and contract. Asset allocation numbers are just numbers. They don't represent judgment or wisdom. As pension fund board members, we are supposed produce the best results for those we serve, instead of slavishly following a set of numbers.

Sometimes, though, it is not that pension fund boards are following a prescribed list showing where to allocate assets. In certain pension funds, the list making is held subordinate to what other pension funds are doing. That is, the board and its consultant will look around in the pension fund world, see that other pension funds are doing this or that, and conclude that they, too, must initiate similar programs. This tendency is another to guard against, because what is right for one pension fund at one point in time might be exactly what is wrong at another point in time or for another pension fund. Let's look at this issue.

People often get caught up in the activities of the moment. They don't think of what is being done, or why. Just because other pension funds do this or that does not make it the right thing to do. The French entomologist, Jean-Henri Fabre, conducted an experiment that drives this point home.

The experiment used processionary caterpillars—wormlike creatures that travel in long, undulating lines, at the same pace and cadence, giving no thought to their final destination. Without forethought, they simply follow their leader.

Dr. Fabre placed a group of these caterpillars onto the thin rim of a large flowerpot. The leader of the group was nose to tail with the last caterpillar in the slow, nonending, deliberate procession. Even for Dr. Fabre, it was impossible to determine which was the leader and which were the followers.

In the center of the flowerpot, Fabre placed an abundant supply of food. The caterpillars paraded around and around, day after day, night after night, until after seven days and nights, the caterpillars began to die off one by one. They died of starvation and utter exhaustion. The abundant supply of food was only a few inches away, but slightly outside the path they traveled. Their source of life was visible but not available unless they altered their habitual and instinctive processionary process.[2]

Why is it that so often we act mindlessly without regard for our circumstances, just because everyone else is acting mindlessly? As circumstances change, we don't purposefully deal with those changes. Many of the most fundamental concepts in pension fund investing were developed decades ago and have served us reasonably well ever since. In the intervening years, however, conditions have changed. What was once valid enough to have served us well then needs purposeful revision now.

The baby-boom population explosion created huge pension liabilities. When these liabilities were many decades away, board members could afford to believe that their investment horizons were unlimited. Now that these liabilities have become shorter term, pension fund board members must make preparations to pay the pensions. The effect of the baby boom stretches from the present to 50 years into the future. In reality, teachers of the baby-boomers are *already* beginning to retire in great numbers, and many of them will live on their pensions for another 20 to 30 years.

This means that while the pension funds have considered themselves as the ultimate long-term investors, they have actually been multiple-horizon investors, with different size groups of people generating obligations with different investment horizons. And, because of demographics, the largest group of pension plan participants are moving closer to retirement, and investments made on their behalf must admit this reality. We cannot act as though the pension liabilities of the 1940s and '50s are the same as those of the 1990s and the 2000s.

---

[2]Glen Van Ekeren, *The Speaker's Sourcebook*, © 1998. Reprinted by permission of the publisher, Prentice Hall/A Division of Simon & Schuster, Englewood Cliffs, N.J.

Fortunately, unlike processionary caterpillars, board members can call upon their wisdom and foresight to exercise wise stewardship of the assets entrusted to them. They can look to their obligations and their other circumstances and decide for themselves how to meet the needs of their fund.

Responsible stewardship cannot be defined in one fell swoop. It is especially hard to distill the practice of responsible stewardship into a set of rules to be followed blindly because nothing about stewardship can be done blindly. Honest and well-intentioned board members may use a single set of facts and come to different conclusions about how to best discharge their stewardship responsibilities. Still, pension fund boards face other kinds of special challenges in their efforts to be good stewards.

One such challenge occurs when the urge to agree overcomes our ability to stand up for what is sensible and moral. Whether this desire plays itself out against a backdrop of indifference, fatigue, or merely the desire to go along with the rest of the crowd, it is a dangerous practice to get into. The peculiar thing about the urge to agree is that it is most often based on a *nonexistent* sense of group tyranny. That is, the pressure to agree that we think we feel from other board members may not really exist. Jerry B. Harvey, a professor at George Washington University, has done some fascinating work on this subject. In his book *The Abilene Paradox and Other Meditations on Management*, Professor Harvey explains his observations and conclusions about group behavior by telling us about the Abilene Paradox and the Gunsmoke Phenomenon:

> "That July afternoon in Coleman, Texas (population 5,607), was particularly hot—104 degrees according to the Walgreen's Rexall's thermometer. In addition, the wind was blowing fine-grained West Texas topsoil through the house. But the afternoon was still tolerable—even potentially enjoyable. A fan was stirring the air on the back porch; there was cold lemonade; and finally, there was entertainment. Dominoes. Perfect for the conditions. The game requires little more physical exertion than an occasional mumbled comment, 'Shuffle 'em,' and an unhurried movement of the arm to place the tiles in their appropriate positions on the table. All in all, it had the makings of an agreeable Sunday afternoon in Coleman. That is, until my father-in-law suddenly said, 'Let's get in the car and go to Abilene and have dinner at the cafeteria.' I thought, 'What, go to Abilene? Fifty-three miles? In this dust storm and heat? And in an unairconditioned 1958 Buick?'
>
> But my wife chimed in with, 'Sounds like a great idea. I'd like to go. How about you, Jerry?' Since my own preferences were obviously out of step

with the rest, I replied, 'Sounds good to me,' and added, 'I just hope your mother wants to go.'

'Of course I want to go,' said my mother-in-law. 'I haven't been to Abilene in a long time.'

So into the car and off to Abilene we went. My predictions were fulfilled. The heat was brutal. Perspiration had cemented a fine layer of dust to our skin by the time we arrived. The cafeteria's food could serve as a first-rate prop in an antacid commercial.

Some four hours and 106 miles later, we returned to Coleman, hot and exhausted. We silently sat in front of the fan for a long time. Then, to be sociable and to break the silence, I dishonestly said, 'It was a great trip, wasn't it?'

No one spoke.

Finally, my mother-in-law said, with some irritation, 'Well, to tell the truth, I really didn't enjoy it much and would rather have stayed here. I just went along because the three of you were so enthusiastic about going. I wouldn't have gone if you all hadn't pressured me into it.'

I couldn't believe it. 'What do you mean "you all"?' I said. 'Don't put me in the "you all" group. I was delighted to be doing what we were doing. I didn't want to go. I only went to satisfy the rest of you. You're the culprits.'

My wife looked shocked. 'Don't call me a culprit. You and Daddy and Mama were the ones who wanted to go. I just went along to keep you happy. I would have had to be crazy to want to go out in heat like that.'

Her father entered the conversation with one word: 'Hay-ell.' He then expanded on what was already absolutely clear: 'Listen, I never wanted to go to Abilene. I just thought you might be bored. You visit so seldom I wanted to be sure you enjoyed it. I would have preferred to play another game of dominoes and eat the leftovers in the icebox.'

After the outburst of recrimination, we all sat back in silence. Here we were, four reasonably sensible people who—of our own volition—had just taken a 106-mile trip across a godforsaken desert in furnacelike heat and a dust storm to eat unpalatable food at a hole-in-the-wall cafeteria in Abilene, when none of us had really wanted to go. To be concise, we'd done just the opposite of what we wanted to do. The whole situation simply didn't make sense.

At least it didn't make sense at the time. But since that day in Coleman, I have observed, consulted with, and been a part of more than one organization that has been caught up in the same situation. As a result, the organizations have taken side trips, or occasionally, terminal 'journeys to Abilene,' when Dallas or Houston or Tokyo was where they really wanted to go. And, for most of those organizations, the negative consequences of such trips, measured in terms of both human misery and economic loss, have been much greater than for our little Abilene group.

I now call the tendency for groups to embark on excursions that no group member wants 'the Abilene Paradox.' Stated simply, when organizations blunder into the Abilene Paradox, they take actions in contradiction to what they really want to do and therefore defeat the very purposes they are trying to achieve. Business theorists typically believe that managing conflict is one of the greatest challenges faces by any organization, but a corollary of the Abilene Paradox states that the inability to manage agreement may be the major source of organization dysfunction.

In more practical terms, so long as we can convince ourselves and others that the sinister forces of groupthink prevented us from confronting a controversial issue during a staff meeting or that peer pressure caused our juvenile delinquency, we don't have to accept responsibility for our own behaviors. In fact, we can blame others for all our mortal sins and minor peccadilloes. However, we may be nervous about our absolution, because we know that the fantasy of group pressure doesn't ring quite true.

At least twice a year, some TV program recapitulates an archetypal 'Gunsmoke' plot, in which a poor dirt farmer is riding across the prairie to Dodge City to get provisions for his pregnant wife and their ten bedraggled kids. Eight miles outside of town on a little-used trail, his horse steps into a gopher hole and goes lame. At the same time, the Frickert Gang is robbing the Dodge City Bank. In the process, they murder the teller and steal half the horses in the town to thwart the posse. The varmints escape by the same trail on which the expectant father is waiting forlornly for help. Being greedy, Jesse Frickert, the gang's leader, sells the farmer a stolen horse, which the farmer innocently rides to Dodge City.

Immediately upon arrival, the farmer is arrested by Marshal Dillon. The marshal charges him with horse theft, murder, and bank robbery, which— as you probably know—are not misdemeanors. Dillon always throws the poor fellow in jail, but from his cell the guy stoutly contends that he is blameless. Dillon always tends to believe him. Saying that he has heard that the man has a good reputation in the county, the marshal speculates that a jury probably will find him innocent.

Unfortunately, though, the judge is out of town. (He always seems to be in Pecos at a convention, and it always seems to take him a minimum of five days to ride back to conduct the trial.) So Dillon explains that the man will have to wait in jail until the judge returns to release him. 'Assuming that you are innocent,' Dillon says, 'and I believe that you probably are, the jury will acquit you, and we will get Doc Adams out in time to tend to the missus and to deliver number eleven. I'm going to have to lock you up until then, but don't worry. This is a fair, law-abiding town, and assuming that you ain't lying, everything's going to turn out all right.'

Then night comes, and you know as well as I what happens. A mob forms at the local saloon—in this case, the Longbranch. Someone shouts, 'Let's hang him. Ain't no need for waiting for no dumb circuit judge to get back from carousing around in Pecos. We caught him dead to rights, so let's string him up, get it over with, and get this town back on an even keel.'

And just as suddenly, everyone breaks for their ropes. There is always a tearful scene played out somewhere as one member of the potential mob gallops up to his house on his trusty steed. He suddenly pulls up the reins, his horse plants its haunches, and he begins to dismount as they slide to the hitching post in a cloud of dust. The rider whips the reins around the post, runs into the house, and shouts to his sleepy wife, who—though just aroused from a deep slumber—is always starched and prim in her nightgown: 'Lou Ann, whar's my rope?'

'What do you want a rope for, Sam? Have the cattle broke out?'

'Woman, just help me find my rope and don't ask no questions!'

'But Sam, I don't understand why you need a rope in the middle of the night. Are the horses loose?'

'The horses ain't loose, but your jaw's going to be loose if you don't quit your yammering. Just shut up and help me find my rope.'

And then it dawns on her what is really happening. 'Oh, Sam,' she says— as she grabs hold of him, 'you ain't a-gonna hang him, are you? Oh, please don't. It ain't fair. He deserves a fair trial. Think of our kids, Sam. How can you ever look 'em in the eye if you do it? Please don't—for my sake. Oh God, Sam, I'm begging you . . . please.'

But before she can finish her sentence, Sam pushes her away and grabs the rope, which has been in plain view all along. As he mounts his horse and rides toward the open prairie, he mumbles to her in a half-incomprehensible voice, 'I don't want to do it, but everyone else does.'

After essentially the same scene is played out at various locations in the area, a mob assembles at the Longbranch and begins what is called the 'torchlight parade' up Main Street. They head toward the jail, which also doubles as the marshal's office.

Dillon, vaguely aware that something is amiss, is always squinting around the shutter that covers the front window. As it dawns on him what is happening, he turns to Festus, his chief confidant and the equivalent of the administrative assistant in contemporary organizations. Dillon shouts, 'Festus, a mob is heading this way from the Longbranch. Take a shotgun, stand by the cell, and try to hold 'em off if they get through the front door. I'll go out and see if I can cool 'em off.'

At this moment, we, the viewers of this mythological event portrayed on our TV, are saying, 'Look at that. A riot. One solitary man aligned in lonely conflict against the tyrannical forces of an irrational mob. It reminds me of what goes on at my office. Can Dillon hold out?'

The question seems legitimate enough. Unknown to us, though, as we interpret the conflict as individuality versus mob rule, we are subtly training ourselves and others to believe in the negative fantasy of group tyranny. In turn, the more we believe that fantasy, the more likely we are to use conformity pressures as excuses for failing to act with courageous integrity in other organizational settings.

Then . . . Marshal Dillon steps out the door of the jail. I'm always amazed at what happens.

Five hundred burly men are assembled in the street. They have wagons, pistols, shotguns, rifles, torches, ropes, knives, signs, whiskey, horses, mules, telegraph poles, sledgehammers, and horsewhips. In addition, small boys are peering from beneath every porch and doorstep in the vicinity. Likewise, women of all ages are peeking between the curtains from every candle-lit room that fronts on the main street of town.

Despite the chaos and scrutiny, Dillon steps forward and—in a calm, nonchalant, nearly insouciant voice—says, 'Howdy.'

Someone in the crowd always replies, 'Howdy, Marshal. Nice night, ain't it?' (This is called the 'introductory palaver'; it is a necessary prelude for the second phase of the ritual encounter, which aficionados term 'the escalation.')

'Marshal, you know why we are here.'

'I know why you're here,' Dillon replies, 'but there ain't gonna be any hanging tonight. This star (as he taps the gilded badge that glitters above his left shirt pocket) says everybody in this town gets a fair chance. So get back to the Longbranch, to your drinking and cardplaying and women. You'll get your day in court.'

And once again we viewers say, 'What tyranny! What conflict! What conformity pressures! One solitary man standing alone against a crazed mob. Peer pressure at its worst. Can Dillon hold out?'

Then someone shouts, 'We ain't here to hassle you, Marshal, but we're a-gonna hang him.'

Dillon replies, 'And I'm not here to hassle you, either, but nobody's coming in this jail.'

To which an unshaven man wearing a dusty black hat responds, 'If that's the way you want it, that's the way you're a-gonna get it. Step aside, Marshal, 'cause here we come.'

The mob surges forward and we tube-viewers say, 'Dillon is in real trouble. They are going to get him for sure.'

But after three steps, the deep voice of our beloved marshal booms forth: 'Hold it right where you are. You see this line on the ground, fellows?' And he scratches a line about four feet long with the heel of his boot.

'We see it, Marshal.'

'First person to step across it gets his head blown off.'

There is a lengthy silence, and then someone in the crowd says, 'Well, if you put it that way,' and the crowd slowly disappears.

At the same time, we couch potatoes say to one another, 'What a hero! One individual, aligned in lonely conflict against the primitive forces of group tyranny and mob rule, faced them eyeball-to-eyeball and they blinked. What courage!'

[Dillon's] courage came from running the risk of helping the people in the mob do exactly what they wanted to do from the start—to extricate themselves from the situation without too much loss of face. In metaphorical terms, he helped avert a trip to Abilene, because the townsfolk didn't really want to hang anyone. In addition, as a marshal, he didn't want to let the prisoner be hanged, for reasons of both justice and practicality. Just imagine the reports, red tape, and paperwork that a lynching might cause. And the potential hangee would be against it, I suspect, for a variety of reasons.

[But] if group tyranny is an overrated notion, is Marshal Dillon any less courageous? A Marshal Dillon devoid of the myth of group tyranny is still courageous to face the existential risk that affiliation, justice, good sense, and love are more characteristic of any given group than alienation, injustice, irrationality, and hate. Before making his moral and sensible stand, Marshal Dillon can only estimate how likely it is that a bullet from Billy Bob's .44 will make a ventilation hole above the Marshal's navel.

If you can't accept the possibility of the worst that could happen if you behave sensibly, regardless of how small that possibility may be, then you have to suffer the ravages of group tyranny. Paradoxically, you have to suffer them even if such tyranny is only mythical. Or, in the Gunsmoke metaphor, if you can't accept the risk of a bullet in the stomach, you have to open the jail door, collude with the mob in sacrificing an innocent victim, [and] blame your actions on group tyranny."[3]

In the investment world, people go to Abilene all too often. The strong urge to "go along—get along" has deep roots in all humans beings,

[3]Jerry B. Harvey, *The Abilene Paradox and Other Meditations on Management* (Lexington, MA: Lexington Books, 1988), pp. 13–15, 107–21.

who depend on social cooperation for our very survival. When people gather to make decisions, there is a group dynamic at work. Nobody wants to look foolish or embarrass themselves in front of others. This would cause them to become outcasts for having expressed their dissent from the group's apparent collective will. In the pension fund world, often individuals will advocate decisions that promote a narrowly focused proposal which may or may not be in everyone's best interest. The easy thing to do is to support this type of proposal when it seems like everyone else is in favor. The urge to agree is powerful. Yet, by agreeing to do what you think everyone else wants to do may be precisely the wrong thing to do. And, doing the wrong thing will not benefit either yourself or the pension fund.

At other times, there may be a choice between alternatives. In this case, amazingly, despite all concrete evidence to the contrary, whoever makes the first motion to approve one or the other alternative can often carry the day, simply by giving the other members of the group something to agree on. Many pension fund investment and actuarial decisions are made in this fashion. And, in and of itself, coming to an agreement is not a bad thing. It is coming to a decision that nobody really wants, simply because we are afraid of the prospect of potential group censure that is the real danger.

For the board member, the essence of the Abilene Paradox and the Gunsmoke Phenomenon is easy to describe. Yet, in practice, the emotional tug each one of us feels in confronting the urge to agree is difficult to resist. As stewards, pension fund board members are held to a higher standard of behavior than others. What is this higher standard? Simply this: The interests of the beneficiaries must come first. When board members are asked to make a decision, the first call to order is to ask themselves a deceptively simple question: How will this decision help us pay the pensions?

Pension fund stewards must first answer this question, or responsible decision making is impossible. If we are unwilling to face down the apparently unruly mob, we might as well get in the Buick and head straight to Abilene.

## MINDFUL ACTION AND COLLECTIVE PURPOSE

From time to time, board members get overwhelmed with the constant demands made on their time and attention. Over time, the flow of information can induce a profound feeling of indifference to the hard work of stewardship. This indifference can be dangerous to pension fund board members. This point was driven home to me recently by an unlikely source.

While near my upstate hometown recently, I went to see the old family barber, Jake. Jake's Barber Shop is located on Routes 6 and 11, in the town of Chinchilla, Pennsylvania. There is nothing extraordinary about the shop. It has two chairs for cuttin' and groomin' and a bunch of chairs against the wall to accommodate customers waiting their turn. Yet there is something special here, and that's Jake. Jake is a big, warm, loquacious Italian with a smile, a story, and a bit of advice for every patron—all for the price of a $5 haircut.

It was a drizzly Thursday as I pulled up to Jake's. My mood was reflective of the weather. Seems I was wrestling with the world's indifference and I wasn't winning. For the love of life, I just couldn't get the message across: indifference is a silent killer. To make matters worse, nobody seemed to care. When I walked in, Jake said: "Hey, C.B. How you doing, buddy? I'll be finished here in a minute, and you're next."

"I'm OK, Jake," I said.

Jake picked up immediately on my foul mood. As I stepped up to the chair, he noted, "C.B., I can see something is bothering you. A little trim, a good listening, and a bit of my advice tonic will put a whole new face on matters."

"Jake," I said as I sat down, "the world is overdosed on indifference. How can I explain to folks that it is a dangerous attitude? When people don't give a damn, they begin to die. How can I make people understand?"

After a moment, he spoke, "C.B., what do you know about frogs?"
"Jake," I countered, "precious little. But who cares about frogs?"

But Jake knew better, and continued on. "C.B., bear with me. I think I know what you mean about indifference. So let me explain." And as he cut my hair, Jake told me the following peculiarity about frogs: "You see," he said, "frogs are reptiles. They adapt their body temperature to their surroundings. If you place a frog in boiling water, it tries like the dickens to jump out as fast as it can. However, if you place a frog in cool water and slowly bring it to a boil, the frog won't ever jump out. Before long, you'll have frog soup. Little by little, the frog adjusts itself to the temperature of the water until it boils to death."

Jake was right. Why is it that people will try like the dickens to jump out of hot water, but remain indifferent to seemingly minor negative changes in circumstance? As nobody seems immune from this problem, we must try to combat indifference by recognizing the beguiling nature of our desire to adapt. Board members must remember that adaptation is essential to survival, but only when it serves the greater good. When we go along to get along, be careful. Otherwise, we can be led into a myriad of minor compromises that, when taken together, can lead to ruin.

If indifference can be a problem, it is one we must try to combat individually. The board as a whole has other problems that need to be tackled together by their very nature. But the board must have an agreement on how to approach these issues collectively. This type of an agreement is known as a social contract. We may not all agree on this point or that one, but as board members, we have a responsibility to attempt to agree on some of the larger issues. There is a good example of a social contract each of us who drives encounters virtually every time we get behind the wheel.

As we go down the road, we see a stop sign that says to us in effect, "You will now come to a stop." We, as licensed drivers, agree that when we see a stop sign, we will stop. These signs are indispensable for the smooth functioning of traffic. Without stop signs, intersections would be chaotic. When individuals come to a stop sign, they agree to stop. They agree to do so even if they would prefer driving through the intersection and not be bothered to stop. Why? Because if they don't stop, they might get into an accident and hurt themselves or others. Stop signs are perfect examples of functioning social contracts. Individuals give up certain of their rights in order that society as a whole will benefit.

Society is composed of both individual and collective interests. These two are often in conflict with each other. Society cannot function without both implicit and explicit social contracts to reconcile and mediate conflict. Typically, society interferes with individual rights in order to pursue the agreed-upon greater common goal. With stop signs, the greater goal is safety. The right of an individual to go through an intersection is curtailed to permit safe entry and exit through the intersection by everyone.

Pension funds (particularly public or union pension funds) are usually governed by boards consisting of groups of individual board members, each working to benefit their own interest and that of their constituency. Yet there is a greater common goal at hand among the members of a board. That greater common goal is best expressed in the central credo of pension fund stewardship: The beneficiaries and their pension benefits must come first.

This might not appear to be such a radical notion. Yet some pension fund board members might say this message is too simple to be of any practical use and that following this simple credo in times of board conflict is impractical. Yet it is especially during these times of conflict that it becomes most important to act in the interest of the common good. Conflict provides opportunities to exercise mature and wise stewardship through an understanding of the social contract. In fact, it is precisely in the heat of battle where it is *most* important to refuse to go along with proposals that seem harmful to the best interests of the beneficiaries. In these cases, board members must try to find the courage to give up the natural inclination to agree with a flawed consensus and put forth an argument supporting a decision on behalf of the greater good, seeking one another's cooperation in the effort.

The element of cooperation cannot be underestimated in the formation of successful social contracts. The following story illustrates this point well:

> A troop of boy scouts gathered for their annual hike in the woods. Taking off at sunrise, they commenced a 15-mile trek through some of the most scenic grounds in the country. About mid-morning, the scouts came across an abandoned section of railroad track. Each, in turn, tried to walk the narrow rails, but after only a few unsteady steps, each lost his balance and tumbled off.
>
> Two of the scouts, after watching one after another fall off the iron rail, offered a bet to the rest of the troop. The two bet that they could both walk the entire length of the railroad track without falling off even once.
>
> The other boys laughed and said, "No way!" Challenged to make good their boast, the two boys jumped up on opposite rails, simply reached out and held hands to balance each other, and steadily walked the entire section of track with no difficulty.[4]

Cooperation in the service of the greater good is never easy, as board politics inevitably involve a certain amount of gamesmanship. Competing interests vie for ascendency as the board moves through its decision-making process. Yet, just as at an intersection in the road, if there is no agreement, no stop sign, it is possible for someone to get hurt. With a pension fund, that someone is usually the beneficiary.

---

[4]Glenn Van Ekeren, *The Speaker's Sourcebook* (Englewood Cliffs, N.J.: Prentice Hall, 1988).

## MOORINGS

With pension assets approaching $3 trillion in 1991, they have become
the obvious targets of much mischief, both from corporations and from
politicians. With so much money at stake, everyone wants to divert pension
assets into activities unrelated to paying pension benefits.

The Employee Retirement Income and Security Act of 1974 (ERISA)
governs private-sector pension funds. Public sector pension systems fall
under the jurisdiction of the states and municipalities in which they operate.
ERISA states that assets of a pension fund be managed "for the exclusive
benefit of the plan's beneficiaries." This reasonable and prudent provision
is commonly referred to as the exclusive benefit rule and has been adopted
by many non-ERISA funds operating in the public sector.

The exclusive benefit rule has come under attack from several sides.
The corporate argument was made by Douglas Love in *Barron's:*

> To identify the economic ownership of pension plan assets, it is sufficient
> to identify how the risks and rewards of their investment are borne. . . . In
> a defined benefit plan it is the company stockholders who are on the hook
> for investment performance. . . . Employee benefits are defined indepen-
> dently of the performance of plan assets, and employees are therefore in the
> position of bondholders. Bondholders are not owners until and unless the
> firm defaults.[5]

On the face of it, this argument appears reasonable. Yet, let's explore
the issue. Most people will agree that a defined benefit contract should
make plan participants closer to *secured* bondholders than to *unsecured*
bondholders. Secured bondholders have a security interest in the assets of
the plan. This means that the employee and the corporation have agreed
to defer compensation into a special pool of assets intended to back up the
promises to pay the pensions when due. Secured fixed-income indenture
agreements usually have covenants that set standards for a corporate borrower. In the case of a defined benefit plan, it only seems fair that one
of the covenants should be to leave all plan assets in the hands of the plan
so that the bondholders can be assured of being paid. In fact, a better
illustration might be to think of a pension plan as a sinking fund established
to ensure prompt payment in full of pension liabilities. In this case, plan

[5]Douglas A. Love, "Who Owns America's Pension Assets? Why Care?" *Barron's National Business and Financial Weekly*, November 19, 1990, p. 28.

participants become secured bondholders with a first claim on a pool of assets designed to pay benefits. Still, a corporation might argue that surplus assets belong to the corporation, not to the plan itself, to be managed for the exclusive benefit of the plan participants. Again, this might seem reasonable at first glance. Yet, we must remember that both asset values *and* corporate fortunes go up *and* down over the course of time.

Plan assets deemed to be in surplus at one point in time, under one set of market conditions and actuarial assumptions, may be needed to pay pensions if conditions change for the worse. What's more, corporate fortunes also wax and wane, changing the ability to increase future contributions to pay pensions. And recent reports show that the Pension Benefit Guaranty Corporation, the insurance fund covering corporate pension plans, is not equipped to handle more than a few large claims simultaneously. The best course is to leave *all* plan assets in the plan to assure participants of benefit payments.

Public pension funds are not subject to the ERISA laws. Nevertheless, these plans usually have similar exclusive benefit rules. But the exclusive benefit rule is no more popular with politicians than it is with corporate chieftains. The argument of the politicians is that public plans are funded with public monies, and therefore the assets don't really belong to the plan itself to be managed for the exclusive benefit of the plan participants, but are owned by the state or municipality. If there is a shortfall in plan assets, the argument goes, the state or municipality can simply raise taxes to pay pensions. However, as discussed earlier, it is unrealistic to believe that politicians can raise taxes at will. As we all know, there are many constraints to tax increases.

What's more, public fund board members have an obligation to manage assets prudently, thereby driving down the cost of funding and saving taxpayers' money. This fiduciary obligation of public fund board members is often overlooked but of vital importance.

In the public sector, social investing tempts politicians. This practice uses pension assets to support projects deemed to be in the public interest. Social investing is both inefficient and unfair, as it places the burden and risks of funding public policy initiatives on the backs of one group of taxpayers, the plan participants. In mid-1989, a report was printed sounding a clarion call for a new wave of social investing by pension funds. This report stated:

> The fiduciaries of today's large pension funds are confronted with a broad array of new needs and constituencies beyond those of retired and current employees. The interests of the employer that sponsors the pension plan,

the needs of the companies in which the fund has invested, and the strength of the national, state, and local economies are all important, *for each can have an impact on the welfare of the pension fund's beneficiaries* (italics added).[6]

Of course, this is a circular proposition. That is, the importance of any nonpension-related need is asserted to be significant only in the context of its positive impact on the beneficiaries. This may relate to the author's underlying ambivalence about his argument. After all, it is hard for anyone to assert that a pension fund should ignore the direct economic needs of the plan participants, so a case is attempted for their indirect needs. Nevertheless, regardless of arguments to the contrary, the direct economic needs of the plan participants must come first.

The touchstone for the board member has *always* been to manage the affairs of the plan to be able to pay the pension benefits when they fall due. This single mission constitutes the beginning, the middle, and the end of pension fund investment strategy. If we seem to have lost our way recently and have developed different guiding principles, a return to common sense is in order.

While there are many forces that compete for a pension fund board member's attention and loyalty, the mission must remain clear and in focus. All the tools of modern portfolio theory, all the efforts of the academicians and statisticians—in short, every resource available to the pension fund—ought to be used in service to this single-minded goal.

No discussion of pension funds would be complete without a mention of the role of the contributors to the funds. Employee and employer contributions form the backbone of any pension plan. These contributions represent a form of compensation to plan participants. Contributions are not a gift from a governmental entity or from a corporation. They are part of the earnings of those who work, whether deducted from a paycheck or contributed from another source. Accordingly, these contributions, and the earnings on these contributions, constitute property of the plan itself to be managed for the exclusive benefit of the plan participants and must be controlled and governed accordingly. Once pension fund contributions have been made, they belong to the plan, not to the contributors. Moreover, it is morally indefensible to assert that someone else's property should be

---

[6]Lee Smith, ed., *Our Money's Worth: A Report of the Governor's Task Force on Pension Fund Investment* (New York: New York State Industrial Cooperation Council, 1989).

managed without the owner's informed consent. Since few, if any, plan participants would consent to anything that would place their pensions in jeopardy, board members must be especially careful to remain good stewards. Given these facts, it is only once the primary mission of a pension fund is fully assured that any other factors can be considered in the investment of pension assets.

Managing the financial affairs of others is never an easy task. There are few rewards for success, and severe penalties for failure. We hope this short book contributes to the ability of board members to succeed in the proper discharge of their duties as stewards. It is an important task and a thankless one. Good luck and Godspeed.

# APPENDIX

## SUMMARY REPORT OF HURDLE-RATE CALCULATIONS PREPARED FOR THE PENNSYLVANIA PUBLIC SCHOOL EMPLOYES' RETIREMENT SYSTEM

This report was the frontispiece of the original report on integration of the actuarial and investment objectives of the Pennsylvania Public School Employes' Retirement System during the tenure of Mr. Clay Mansfield as the chief investment officer of the system. While the full report is far too extensive and tedious to be presented here, the summary is shown below.

### SUMMARY OF STUDY

This report summarizes the results of the cash flow study for the Pennsylvania Public School Employes' Retirement System under various forecast alternatives for the 10-year projection period from July 1, 1985, through June 30, 1995.

A description of the various forecast alternatives and the assumptions used to prepare them is presented below.

### OBJECTIVES OF STUDY

The objectives of the cash flow study may be summarized as being twofold:

1. To develop the liquidity requirement, or net cash flows, of the system for the next 10 years.

2. To determine the funding target, or real economic liability, of the system at the end of the 10-year projection period.

The funding target is defined as being the termination liability of the system at the end of the 10-year projection period, that is, that amount of assets that will be exactly sufficient at the end of the 10-year projection period to provide the total accrued pension benefits of the active and retired membership if the system were to be terminated.

This asset target was determined using an interest rate of 5½ percent, which is consistent with the interest rate required to be used by the statute of the Commonwealth for the traditional actuarial valuation of the system.

## PROJECTION ASSUMPTIONS

As a preliminary step to the cash flow study, we completed a five-year review of the experience of the system for the fiscal years 1981 through 1985. The results of this review are contained in Section V of the Schedule of Results.

Based upon these experience results, we revised the current actuarial assumptions so that the cash flow projections would more closely approximate the recent experience of the system. The actuarial assumptions used in completing the projections are summarized in Section IV of the Schedule of Results and can be found at page 27 of the Schedule.

## DESCRIPTION OF SCENARIOS

### Scenarios A, B, and C

Financial forecasts were first prepared on the basis of three scenarios identified as Scenario A, Scenario B, and Scenario C. These three scenarios were designed to test the sensitivity of the cash flow of the system and the 10-year target liability to changes in the level of early and superannuation retirement and annual pay increases of the membership.

Scenario A was completed using a moderate set of retirement rates and future annual pay increases of 7 percent. The results of the financial forecast under Scenario A are summarized in Tables I to IV, which can be found at pages 1 through 5 of the Schedule of Results.

To test the impact of a sharp increase in the rate of retirement, we increased the rates of retirement under Scenario A by 25 percent. We then completed a projection on this revised basis referred to as Scenario B, which can be found at pages 6 through 10 of the Schedule of Results. An acceleration of retirements as modeled under Scenario B could be brought about by the introduction of employer-paid post-retirement medical benefits.

To complete the initial series of projections, we revised the annual pay assumption under Scenario B from 7 percent annually to 9 percent. Using the combination of accelerated retirement under Scenario B and the revised pay assumption of 9 percent, we completed a further projection, which is referred to as Scenario C. The result of this scenario can be found at pages 11 through 15 of the Schedule of Results.

Thus, in regard to the retirement and pay assumptions used, the initial series of projections may be characterized as follows:

Scenario A: Moderate retirement—moderate pay (7 percent).

Scenario B: Accelerated retirement (25 percent increase over Scenario A) moderate pay (7 percent).

Scenario C: Accelerated retirement (25 percent increase over Scenario A) high pay (9 percent).

## Scenarios A–1, B–1, and C–1

Under the model used for Scenarios A, B, and C, employer contributions would decline in line with the schedules implicit in the July 1, 1985, actuarial valuation of the system.

A second series of projections was prepared to measure the effect on cash flows and target liability based on the assumption that employer contributions would remain constant for the entire 10-year projection period at their highest ever level of 20.04 percent.

In effect, Scenarios A, B, and C were revised, using for this second series an employer contribution rate fixed at 20.04 percent during the 10-year projection period. This second series of scenarios are labeled Scenario A–1, B–1, and C–1, with the A–1, B–1, and C–1 labels indicating the results of the respective Scenarios A, B, and C with the contribution rate fixed at 20.04 percent.

## Scenarios A–2, B–2, and C–2

A third series of scenarios was prepared to project the impact of using market value in lieu of book value for the beginning asset value of the projection. As of July 1, 1985, the beginning point of the projection, market value exceeded book value by $463 million.

This third series of projections involved repeating Scenarios A, B, and C, but using market value for this series. The third additional scenarios are identified as Scenarios A–2, B–2, and C–2.

# DESCRIPTION OF PROJECTION OUTPUT

The projection results are presented in the Schedule of Results, which immediately follows.

## Scenarios A, B, and C

For each of these scenarios, Section I of the Schedule of Results presents the following output:

Table I—Annual cash flow.

Table II—New retirees each year.

Table III—Active membership split by new members.

Table IV—10-year hurdle investment rate of return.

## Scenarios A–1, B–1, and C–1

For each of these scenarios, Section I of the Schedule of Results presents the following output:

Table I—Annual cash flow.

Table IV–10-year hurdle investment rate of return.

In each of these scenarios, the output for (a) new retirees each year and (b) active membership split by new members would remain the same as shown in Tables II and III for the respective scenarios A, B, and C.

## Scenarios A–2, B–2, and C–2

For each of these scenarios, Section III of the Schedule of Results presents the following output:

Table IV—10-year hurdle investment rate of return.

In each of these scenarios, output for (a) annual cash flow, (b) new retirees each year, and (c) active membership split by new members would remain the same as shown in Tables I, II and, III for the respective Scenarios A, B, and C.

# PROJECTION RESULTS

The objectives of the financial forecast study were to (i) project the liquidity of the system as shown in Table I (Annual Cash Flow) and (ii) determine the hurdle rate of investment return necessary to achieve the target rate of 100 percent for termination funding as shown in Table IV.

Thus, Table I and Table IV for each scenario show the principal results of the projection study.

The following table presents a comparison of the rate of investment return required to achieve the funding target of 100 percent of the 10-year termination liability under each scenario:

**Hurdle Rate of Investment Return to Achieve System Termination Funding Target**

| Item | Annual Hurdle Rate of Return |
|---|---|
| Scenario A | 10.8% |
| Scenario A-1 | 10.5% |
| Scenario A-2 | 10.2% |
| Scenario B | 10.9% |
| Scenario B-1 | 10.5% |
| Scenario B-2 | 10.3% |
| Scenario C | 11.9% |
| Scenario C-1 | 11.5% |
| Scenario C-2 | 11.4% |

## TERMINATION LIABILITY AS OF JULY 1, 1985

In addition to determining the projected termination liability at the end of the 10-year projection period (i.e., as of June 30, 1995) for each of the scenarios, we have also determined the termination liability if the system were to be terminated at the beginning of the projection period (i.e., as of July 1, 1985) together with the funded status on that date.

The funded status on July 1, 1985, has been determined on the basis of the comparison between (i) the termination liability as of July 1, 1985, using a valuation interest rate of 5½ percent per annum and (ii) the assets of the system as of July 1, 1985, at cost value, as indicated in the following table:

**Funded Status as of July 1, 1985**

| Item | Termination Liability ($ millions) |
|---|---|
| Termination liability | |
| Active membership | $ 8,924.5 |
| Retired membership | 4,950.8 |
| Total | $14,875.3 |
| Assets at cost value: | $ 7,992.8 |
| Funded status: (2) / (1) | 57.6% |

The funded status as of July 1, 1985, is a relevant item in evaluating the significance of the projection results. It shows that, if the funded status of the system is to be raised from the current position of 57.6 percent to 100 percent at the end of 10 years, the system would have to average an annual rate of investment return varying between 10.3 percent and 11.9 percent, depending on the scenario of events. This range in the hurdle rate of investment return is shown in a summary table in this report.

# GLOSSARY

---

*The terms defined below, as used in the text of this book, apply to the world of pension fund investing. There are many other circumstances where stewardship of assets on behalf of others is important. The boards of university endowment funds, foundations, and similar organizations all face problems and challenges requiring the judicious exercise of stewardship. Regardless of this fact, the terms defined below address only the world of pension fund investing and have not been allowed to assume wider possible meanings.*

**applied asset allocation**   The process of allocating assets to asset classes that provide the highest probability of funding current and future pension benefits.

**applied modern portfolio theory**   The use of modern statistical techniques to design a portfolio to achieve the specific financial objective of funding pension liabilities.

**basic pension equation**   The equation related to every pension fund:
Benefit payments = (Contributions − Expenses) + (Investment income)

**cash coverage ratio**—For any given period of time, the cash coverage ratio is the percentage of pension benefit payments that can be covered by cash and cash equivalents without causing a decline in either the funded ratio or an increase in contributions.

**cash flow liability risk**   The risk that a pension fund will have insufficient cash flow to pay its pension obligations.

**cash planning period**   The period covered by a cash plan developed by a pension fund to use interest payments and principal repayments from fixed-income securities to pay current and future pension benefits when and as they fall due during the plan period.

**emergency cash plan**   The plan developed by a pension fund to have on hand a sufficient cash cushion to meet unexpected and unanticipated cash requirements. Emergency cash requirements are cash amounts that cause the cash coverage ratio to exceed 100 percent.

**equity importance**   The importance of stocks in a pension fund portfolio. Because of their higher historic returns, stocks should be used as the assets of choice to cover pension benefit liabilities associated with younger and nonvested plan participants.

**fixed-income importance**   The importance of fixed-income securities in a pension fund portfolio. For reasons of safety and cash flow, fixed-income securities are the assets of choice to cover pension benefit liabilities associated with older and retired plan participants.

**funded ratio** or **funded status**   The amount of assets now on hand divided by the present value of projected liabilities.

**funding risk**   The risk that, for whatever reason, insufficient contributions will be made to fully fund pension benefits.

**funding the benefit**   A conscious decision on the part of a pension fund to structure its portfolio to be able to recognize and pay specific pension benefit obligations as they fall due.

**Harris matrix**   A tool to evaluate and select investment managers (see Chapter 6, Table 6–1).

**hurdle rate of return** or **required rate of return**   That rate of return necessary over a specified period of time to fully fund current and anticipated future pension obligations. Used as a balance sheet integration device that helps determine the degree of attractiveness of an equity sale, and as a device to relate capital market investment choices with a pension fund's balance sheet.

**investment discipline**   The ability to develop, maintain, monitor, and adapt an investment strategy tied to a specific financial objective.

**measured steps**   A simple, uncomplicated approach to investing, based on compounding that seeks to make small, continual gains with fewer mistakes as opposed to seeking brilliantly executed, high-risk, high-return gains.

**mission statement**   The defined role and purpose of a specific pension fund as determined by its body politic.

**multiple-horizon investor**   An investor, such as a pension fund, which requires the realized proceeds from its portfolio on many different dates. Pension funds must pay benefits in the near term, the medium term, and the long term. They are therefore referred to as multiple-horizon investors.

**owner risk**   The risk that the assets owned by a pension fund suffer losses or that the pension fund suffers a lower overall rate of return than its hurdle rate of return.

**performance**    The level of attainment reached by a pension fund in its effort to fully fund and pay both its current and future pension obligations at the lowest level of cost and risk.

**performance measurement**    The degree to which all current and future pension obligations are paid in cash whenever they fall due, as measured by reductions in the hurdle rate of return, reductions in the contribution rate, reductions in the unfunded accrued pension liabilities, and maintenance of a cash coverage ratio in excess of 100 percent.

**rebalancing period**    The annual exercise during which a pension fund reappraises its assets and liabilities with the objective of allocating assets to meet pension liabilities.

**risk**    Risk is a function of the consequence of loss.

**risk measurement**    For a pension fund, risk is measured by the effect produced by investment behavior on a plan's cash planning period, cash coverage ratio, funded ratio, and cost of funding.

**sell discipline**    A strategy to sell assets in a premeditated fashion to meet the financial objective related to paying all current and future pension obligations when and as they fall due.

**single horizon investor**    An investor who requires realization of the full amount of an investment on a specified date. (See **multiple horizon investor**.)

**stewardship**    Managing the affairs of a pension fund to meet the specific financial objectives related to paying all current and future pension obligations when and as they fall due.

**strategic plan**    A comprehensive review of a pension fund's liabilities prepared to develop a series of financial objectives related to paying all current and future pension obligations when and as they fall due.

# INDEX